Living
in a
Man's
World

Lessons I've
Learned
(and Even Some I Haven't)

To order additional copies of *Living in a Man's World,*
by Bonita Joyner Shields, **call 1-800-765-6955.**
Visit us at **www.reviewandherald.com**
for information on other Review and Herald® products.

Bonita Joyner Shields

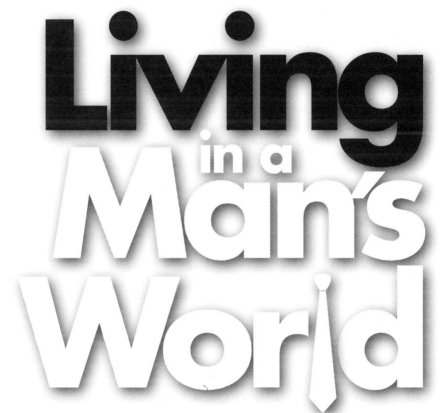

Living
in a
Man's
World

Lessons I've
Learned
(and Even Some I Haven't)

REVIEW AND HERALD® PUBLISHING ASSOCIATION
Since 1861 | www.reviewandherald.com

Review and Herald® titles may be purchased in bulk for educational, business, fund-raising, or sales promotional use. For information, e-mail SpecialMarkets@reviewandherald.com.

The Review and Herald® Publishing Association publishes biblically based materials for spiritual, physical, and mental growth and Christian discipleship.

This book was
Edited by Kalie Kelch
Copyedited by Vesna Mirkovich
Cover designed by Emily Ford / Review and Herald® Design Center
Interior designed by Derek Knecht / Review and Herald® Design Center
Cover art by © Thinkstock.com
Typeset: Minion Pro 11/13

PRINTED IN U.S.A.

17 16 15 14 13   5 4 3 2 1

Library of Congress Cataloging-in-Publication Data
Shields, Bonita Joyner, 1963-
  Living in a man's world : lessons I've learned (and even some I haven't) / Bonita Joyner Shields.
    pages cm
  Includes bibliographical references and index.
  ISBN 978-0-8280-2720-5 (alk. paper)
1. Women clergy. 2. Sex role in the work environment. 3. Gender expression.
4. Man-woman relationships. 5. Church management. I. Title.
BV676.S48 2013
253.082--dc23
                    2013017905

ISBN 978-0-8280-2720-5

Dedication

I dedicate this book to my mother,

Guinevere Hanrahan Joyner,

who taught me that my opinion is just as good as anyone else's,

and my father,

Benjamin Henry Joyner, Sr.
(August 25, 1926–September 25, 1995),

who taught me how to think.

Acknowledgments

It's been said that it takes a village to raise a child. I'd like to suggest that it takes a community to write a book.

From the time this book was birthed in my soul to the final stages of preparation, numerous people have helped along the way:

My Mom: Fortunately, while I was in high school, she impressed upon me two words: *Take typing!* This book would have been much more difficult to write without my having taken my mother's advice.

My Writing Group: The Inking Angels consists of my angelic friends Lyndelle Chiomenti, May-Ellen Colon, Jean Kellner, and Ella Rydzewski. I appreciated their reading through my manuscript, offering suggestions, and encouraging me along the way.

My Reading Committee: Khelsea Bauer, Jennifer Deans, Patty Froese, Betty Kossick, Tim Lale, Sheree Parris Nudd, and Thomas Wetmore read through my manuscript and gave invaluable feedback. Steve Chavez created the dialogue questions at the end of each chapter.

North American Division Leadership: A special thank-you to Debra Brill, vice president, and Ivan Williams, ministerial director, for supporting and endorsing the book in their division of the world church.

Review and Herald Editorial Team: Jeannette Johnson and her team have been great to work with! As a writer and editor, I can be quite picky when it comes to how my writing is edited. However, I am very pleased with how they treated my manuscript.

My Husband: Roy and I have been married for 29 years. I used to think that young married love was the ultimate. Now I think I've changed my mind! The depth of love in this season of our lives is priceless, as is his encouragement of my writing. I don't remember his ever complaining that I was spending too much time writing.

My God: Thank You.

Contents

Foreword

From the fall of Adam and Eve until today, the status of men versus women (or women versus men) has raged as a continuing conflict. Even today the differences that exist in the areas of employment, payment, hours of work required, and church-related ministries cause division. Equality, justice, and Christian fairness often surface as one of the main discussion topics. Author Bonita Joyner Shields, however, does not make this her mantra. Her life revolves around serving her Lord, without conflict, in the denominational environment. She believes that reconciliation is needed in our world, especially in the area of gender relations.

Pastor Shields writes about her experiences being employed by the Seventh-day Adventist Church as a pastor, writer, and editor. As the title of the book suggests, one of the greatest challenges for women surfaces as *living in a man's world*. Bonita does not confront the problems associated with these challenges negatively. She has discovered that when those challenges are confronted with a desire to build bridges of understanding, they can become the source of healing for everyone involved. As I have become acquainted with Bonita, I have begun to realize the challenges that women employed in ministry face often relate to their relationships with the men with whom they work.

Bonita knew when she embraced her calling from God to pastoral ministry many years ago that ordination was not an option. Thus, she asked the Lord to keep her from the resentment that can accompany the absence of that recognition from the church she loves. And she believes the Lord has been faithful in doing that. Her greatest desire is to lead people to understand God and His Word more fully. Ministering to God's people, in whatever form that may take, would be her life's work.

In this volume Bonita expresses her concern regarding the devaluation of women in every culture and profession. However, she encourages us not to allow this to become a battle of "us against them"—women against men. This serves only to enlarge Satan's attempts to divide the genders into opposite and antagonistic groups. She believes—and I agree with her—that men and women have much to learn from each other. One of the most important lessons I learned came to me from a woman. She helped me to understand that "being present" with someone involves much more than my physical presence; it involves truly listening and entering into the experience of that person.

Bonita encourages us to truly listen to the voices of women, and partner with them to spread the gospel to the world more effectively. And since women make up almost 70 percent of the church's membership, why would men not think they should hear the voices of women? We in the North American Division of Seventh-day Adventists are committed to partnering with women to spread the gospel more effectively. Of the approximately 4,000 pastors employed in our division, only 107 are women. The goal of the North American Division is to increase the number of employed female pastors by 100 percent over the next five years. We are also committed to develop intentional methods of mentoring women who can become executive secretaries and treasurers within our conferences.

Bonita speaks strongly about the genders' need to partner with each other. However, she does not want people to think she is encouraging those who are physically and/or emotionally abused to remain silent and not speak up. She could not discuss this topic at length, but chapter 6 offers some helpful guidance for those who believe they may be in an abusive work relationship.

Bonita was fortunate to have the opportunity to work with a leader who was willing to share his influence in order to develop other people's talents and gifts—both male and female. She uses *Living in a Man's World* to affirm and express gratitude for those godly people whom the Lord used throughout her life to encourage her. The North American Division is also eager to implement more of these types of successful working relationships, which include men and women helping each other to succeed. They provide an affirming experience for both genders.

Women who believe they have received from their Lord a calling to ministry should read this account of Pastor Shields' experiences. Men and women, whatever their professions, can also benefit from her insights for strong relationships in the home, the workplace, and the church.

—Ivan L. Williams, Sr., ministerial director
North American Division of Seventh-day Adventists
Silver Spring, Maryland, U.S.A.

To what work
is the Lord leading you?
Pastoral ministry is not
the only work to which
the Lord leads people.
The world needs praying
doctors, faithful businesspersons,
and spirit-filled artists who realize
their calling and who walk
with godly courage.
Is fear, guilt, or shame
keeping you from following
God's leading?

Introduction

Jennifer and I sat at Panera Bread indulging in a fabulous summer salad and even more wonderful conversation. She, a pastor of a local congregation, was sharing with me some of the joys and challenges of her pastoral life and calling. I, a former local pastor now living out my pastoral calling at my church's world headquarters, was sharing with her some of the things I have learned over the years in my life and ministry.

As we were winding down our time together, I shared with her my desire to write a book geared toward intelligent, accomplished Christian women in the workplace—for which she qualifies in all categories. I then asked her what she would like to see in a book such as this. Without having to think long—for she had obviously thought through this already—Jennifer answered: *living in a man's world.*

Her answer prompted me to think back to when I was a local church pastor. I was working on a project with Barbara, one of my church members. As we worked, several pastoral colleagues, who all happened to be male, stopped by to chat with me. After several such encounters, Barbara looked at me and said, "Bonita, you certainly do live in a man's world, don't you?" I had never thought about it before that moment. Of course, as I sat in undergraduate and graduate theology classes, the only female much of the time, I wasn't oblivious to the fact. But I had never expressed it in those terms.

After another pastor friend shared the same sentiment as did Jennifer, it became apparent to me that this theme had been emerging not only in my life but also in the lives of my female friends. So as Jennifer and I parted company that evening, I promised I would think and pray about the topic. We also prayed about it before we said goodbye. I then went home and continued talking to God. "Lord, I've had several books on my heart that I have been wanting to write over the past 10 years, and for some reason I cannot bring them to fruition. If You want me to write this book, I need

You to *give* me the outline!" God is so patient with me. But I think He enjoys it when we hold Him to His word. It was God who brought me into my calling of writing, preaching, and teaching. And I cannot do it without Him.

A few nights later as I sat down to think about this project, I began to write. And within an hour I had my outline written. "OK, Lord," I found myself praying, "You held up Your end of the bargain. Now it's my turn."

So I pressed forward, believing that God was leading me to write this book. The end result of my partnership with God is in your hands. As you read, my hope and desire is that *Living in a Man's World* will accomplish three things.

First, I seek to create a safe place for men and women to have a dialogue about how they can best be partners in the workplace, especially within the church. I want to help break down the wall of "us against them." Thus, you'll notice at the end of each chapter several questions for this purpose.

Second, I seek to build up my Christian sisters as they live out their calling to God's work in a man's world—whatever that calling may be. For while the context of my life is pastoral ministry, and this book flows out of my life's experiences, *Living in a Man's World* is not limited to that context. You may be a professor, doctor, department store supervisor, or businesswoman. Whatever your calling, the challenge is still the same: "How can a woman live in a man's world?" Women do not have to pull men down in order to bring themselves up; that's Satan's counterfeit of the true, authentic, life-giving partnership between men and women.

Third, I seek to answer the question How can a *Christian* woman live in a man's world and be faithful to God, her family, her brothers in Christ with whom she works, and herself? This is one of our greatest challenges of living in a man's world. But if we seek to become instruments of healing, it can become the source of some of our greatest joys. And my greatest desire is that the words of this book will encourage this faithfulness.

Chapter 1

Voices

Lesson: Don't allow your fears to determine your destiny.

Filled with excitement, I carried my box of office paraphernalia to work with me that hot day in July 1995. My dream had come true. I had worked long and hard for this day, writing term papers, completing practicums, passing exams, and praying, a lot! I was ready! Yet as I sat in my office unpacking my "stuff," an overwhelming feeling of fear gripped me. *This is it. I'm a pastor. Am I going to make it?*

My Story

I was 23, perhaps 24, when the Lord began calling me to ministry. A graduate of Washington Adventist University with my associate degree in office administration, I had been married for several years when I decided to take a spiritual gifts class from Bill Liversidge. It changed my life.

We organized into small groups and spent the entire semester discovering our spiritual giftedness within the context of community. In this small community, my classmates and Liversidge planted the seed in my mind that the Lord might be leading me to become a pastor. I listened respectfully. A nice thought—but one that frightened me. *A pastor? I don't think so,* I thought. *Pastors are, well,* special. *You know,* perfect. *And I am far from that. Also, female pastors in the Adventist Church are, well, rare. You know, controversial.* So I shelved the thought and went on with my life.

Several years went by. Then Tim, the youth pastor at our church, asked my husband, Roy, and me whether we would be willing to sit in with him on a Bible study with a young couple, Ed and Cindy. We agreed. Cindy had been an Adventist but had left the church and married while away.

After the second or third study Tim told us he couldn't continue with the study and asked us to lead it. I have no evidence, but I think he planned it that way all along. Who wants to say to their pastor, "Sorry. Not us. The thought scares the daylights out of us! Ed and Cindy will just have to find someone else"? So we agreed.

My schedule being more flexible than Roy's, we decided that I would lead the study. I thrived on the in-depth study and teaching. Halfway through the studies Cindy said to me, "Bonita, I have attended Adventist schools all my life, but I don't remember anyone asking me if I wanted to accept Jesus as my personal Savior. How do I do it?" In the quietness of her kitchen, for the first time in her life, Cindy accepted Jesus as her Lord and Savior.

As Roy and I drove home that night, I said to him, "*Nothing* has ever given me as much joy as leading Cindy to Jesus." Later she, her husband, and their eldest daughter were baptized.

During that time Roy and I were attending prayer meetings at our church. One evening Mike, our senior pastor, rushed through the door before the meeting was to begin and said hastily, "I have an emergency. I can't stay." He looked directly at me and asked, "Bonita, would you lead out tonight?" Who wants to say to her pastor, "Sorry. Not me. It scares the daylights out of me! You'll have to put your emergency on hold or find someone else"? So I agreed. Do you see a pattern here?

Fortunately, the pastor left his notes! I walked nervously to the podium, offered prayer, and led out in the meeting. As I stood there engaging the people in spiritual dialogue, I felt an unusual sense of calm. I experienced one of those rare and beautiful moments in life when a person says to himself or herself, *This is why I was created.*

The pieces to my life's puzzle began fitting together even more when, during one of those Wednesday evening prayer meetings, Erwin Gane, then editor of the *Adult Sabbath School Quarterly,*[1] produced by the General Conference Sabbath School Department, presented on the topic of the Holy Spirit. As he explained the work of the Holy Spirit so articulately and inspirationally, this thought invaded my mind: *This is it! This is what I am to do with my life: lead people to understand God more clearly and help them to understand God's Word and how it relates to their lives.*

Hearing Voices

As I shared with others my decision to return to school to study theology, I heard varied opinions:

"You can't be a pastor; you're a woman."

"I can see you as a teacher but not as a preacher."

Some didn't know what to say, so they remained silent and didn't even acknowledge my decision—for a full seven years.

My natural tendency is to be a people pleaser. So when others expressed their opinions (or didn't express them aloud) based on their beliefs and/ or biases, I internalized those opinions. I feared their disapproval. Thus, I enrolled as a religion major. Studying to become a female religion teacher seemed safer. No controversy.

However, as time went on, I found myself dissatisfied with my program. Something wasn't clicking. I decided to seek the counsel of Charlotte Conway, a woman in leadership at the college whom I highly respected. In the course of our conversation she asked me a simple question: "What is it that you see yourself doing?" As I expressed to her my desires for ministry, she pulled out the college catalog and began browsing. Suddenly she pointed to a page and said to me, "Bonita, here's your program! It fits your vision perfectly: theology with a personal ministries concentration."

I was back where I had started. Be a pastor? Couldn't I live out my calling as a less-controversial figure? I didn't want to be the object of debate by my mere presence. I wanted a work that wouldn't cost so much. I wanted people to like me. I wanted summers off! However, I was not at peace pursuing my current educational track. No matter the cost, it became clear to me that I needed to switch to theology and head into pastoral ministry.

> Courage is not the absence of fear, and courageous acts are not performed by those who feel no fear.

After switching majors that day, I went home and lay on my bed. Suddenly a flood of thoughts about all the things that were wrong in my life washed through my brain. Though not an audible voice, it was a voice nonetheless that said to me sneeringly, *Who do you think you are, trying to be a pastor? You're not good enough.*

It felt as if a 50-pound weight lay on my back. Fortunately, I understood enough about spiritual warfare to know that if I feel guilt with *hope*, it is a godly, redemptive guilt—the Holy Spirit is trying to change something in my life. However, if I feel guilt with *despair and shame*, it is a godless, destructive guilt—Satan is trying to pour salt on the wounds of my sin. That day my feelings of guilt, despair, and shame were far from hopeful.

I cried to God, "Why are You calling me to be a pastor? I'm not good enough. Look at all the wrong things I've done in my life. I don't have the pedigree; my family tree is far from pastoral!" Another voice, not an audible voice but a voice nonetheless, spoke to me. This voice was full of compassion and love. I recognized it. It was my Father's voice. *Bonita, I'm not calling you because you are worthy. I'm calling you because I am worthy!* And with that, the weight of guilt and shame immediately lifted.

For many years fear had kept me from answering God's leading in my life. I feared I wasn't good enough. I feared I didn't know enough. I feared others' opinions of me. But the message God spoke to me that evening has sustained me through many difficult times.

Lord, Give Me Courage

From the beginning of my ministry, the call of the prophet Jeremiah has given me courage:

" 'Before I formed you in the womb I knew you, before you were born I set you apart; I appointed you as a prophet to the nations.'

" 'Alas, Sovereign Lord,' I said, 'I do not know how to speak; I am too young.'

"But the Lord said to me, 'Do not say, "I am too young." You must go to everyone I send you to and say whatever I command you. Do not be afraid of them, for I am with you and will rescue you,' declares the Lord" (Jer. 1:5-8, NIV).

To what work is the Lord leading you? Pastoral ministry is not the only work to which the Lord leads people. The world needs praying doctors, faithful businesspersons, and spirit-filled artists who realize their calling and who walk with godly courage. Is fear, guilt, or shame keeping you from following God's leading?

It takes courage to follow God when we don't feel capable of the task. But what is courage? Courage is not the absence of fear, and courageous acts are not performed by those who feel no fear. Courageous acts are performed by those who choose to move forward despite the fear. As women we often think that we're the only ones who experience fear. But men have fears too. They just don't talk about them as much as we do. One man shared with me that he is afraid of the dark. Vulnerability begets vulnerability. The more we share our fears with one another, the more we will discover that we're not alone. And, ironically, this knowledge of mutually held fear gives power to our lives. It reminds me of 2 Corinthians 1:3, 4: "Praise be to the God and Father of our Lord Jesus Christ, the Father of compassion and the God of all comfort, who comforts us in all our troubles, so that we can comfort those in any trouble with the comfort we ourselves receive from God" (NIV).

God wants us to live not with a spirit of fear but with a spirit of power. Again and again throughout Scripture God comforts us with the words "Do not fear."

But how do we build courage in our lives?

Fear is usually built on false beliefs. Thus, I believe one of the most important things we can do is to change our thinking. Since our thoughts can lie to us, we can begin by asking the question "Do I *know* this to be true?" When we take the time to intentionally ask ourselves this question, more often than not we'll answer no. Dr. Daniel Amen, a psychiatrist, created an excellent step-by-step approach to address this issue. It's called Automatic Negative Thoughts Therapy (ANT Therapy), and he outlines it in an article called "ANT Therapy: How to Develop Your Own Internal Anteater to Eradicate Automatic Negative Thoughts."[2] I've found it very helpful.

Another thing we can do, which I'm sure is not a new idea to you, is to confront those things we fear the most. For example, after a bad car accident, we are encouraged to go back to driving immediately so that we don't allow the fear to become paralyzing. I used to be terrified of driving over bridges. So when I had to do so, I forced myself to look over the side of the bridge at the water—which was at the center of my fear. After much prayer, self-talk, and viewing various bodies of water, I thank the Lord that today I can drive over a bridge without a tinge of fear.

While most of us have some type of fear—big or small—there are times when fear threatens to overwhelm and overcome us. I believe those are direct attacks of Satan. When you experience those moments, I encourage you to ask the Lord to deliver you from Satan's stronghold of fear. One of my prayers regarding fear, taken from a powerful book on spiritual warfare, goes something like this: "Father, I see that fear is not from You. I understand that fear, worry, and doubt are the negative faith of the enemy. Forgive me for doubting Your ability to watch over and care for me. I will trust You from this time forth as my Source of security."[3]

Those aspects of our lives that are the weakest can become, through the power of God's Spirit, our strengths. And those of us who, too often, have allowed fear to determine our destiny can rise above those fears. One of the most meaningful affirmations I've ever received was a friend saying, "Bonita, you're one of the most courageous people I know." I treasure those words.

I overcame the feeling of fear that hot summer day in July 1995. I still experience times that fearful thoughts attempt to keep me from going where God is leading me. *Will I make it? What will people think of me? How will I accomplish what is expected of me? How will I accomplish what I expect of myself?* The challenge still remains not to allow fear to be the determining factor in the choices I make. The difference now, though, is that I know I'm going to make it. I'm learning to listen to the right voice.

---

[1] As of 1998 the name of this publication changed to the *Adult Bible Study Guide.*

[2] Daniel G. Amen, "ANT Therapy: How to Develop Your Own Internal Anteater to Eradicate Automatic Negative Thoughts," AHHA Self-Help Articles Collection, American Holistic Health Association, http://ahha.org/articles.asp?Id=100 (accessed Jan. 13, 2013).

[3] Jerry and Carol Robeson, *Strongman's His Name . . . What's His Game?* (New Kensington, Pa.: Whitaker House, 1984), p. 134.

Dialogue Questions

1. What events in your life have led you to the place you are in now? List at least three.

2. What emotions prevent you from feeling worthy of being used by God? What spiritual truth would counteract those emotions?

3. How do you imagine your future? What do you feel God is calling you to do?

4. What could your life look like if you were to allow God's power and courage rather than fear to determine your destiny?

20 Scripture Quotations on Courage

Deuteronomy 31:6—"Be strong and of a good courage, fear not, nor be afraid of them: for the Lord thy God, he it is that doth go with thee; he will not fail thee, nor forsake thee."

Joshua 1:7-9—"Only be thou strong and very courageous, that thou mayest observe to do according to all the law, which Moses my servant commanded thee: turn not from it to the right hand or to the left, that thou mayest prosper withersoever thou goest. This book of the law shall not depart out of thy mouth; but thou shalt meditate therein day and night, that thou mayest observe to do according to all that is written therein: for then thou shalt make thy way prosperous, and then thou shalt have good success. Have not I commanded thee? Be strong and of a good courage; be not afraid, neither be thou dismayed: for the Lord thy God is with thee whithersoever thou goest."

1 Chronicles 28:20—"And David said to Solomon his son, Be strong and of good courage, and do it: fear not, nor be dismayed: for the Lord God, even my God, will be with thee; he will not fail thee, nor forsake thee, until thou hast finished all the work for the service of the house of the Lord."

Psalm 23:4—"Yea, though I walk through the valley of the shadow of death, I will fear no evil: for thou art with me; thy rod and thy staff they comfort me."

Psalm 27:1—"The Lord is my light and my salvation; whom shall I fear? the Lord is the strength of my life; of whom shall I be afraid?"

Psalm 31:24—"Be of good courage, and he shall strengthen your heart, all ye that hope in the Lord."

Psalm 56:3, 4—"What time I am afraid, I will trust in thee. In God I will praise his word, in God I have put my trust; I will not fear what flesh can do unto me."

Isaiah 41:10-13—"Fear thou not; for I am with thee: be not dismayed; for I am thy God: I will strengthen thee; yea, I will help thee; yea, I will uphold thee with the right hand of my righteousness. Behold, all they that were incensed against thee shall be ashamed and confounded: they shall be as nothing; and they that strive with thee shall perish. Thou shalt seek them, and shalt not find them, even them that contended with thee: they that war against thee shall be as nothing, and as a thing of nought. For I the Lord thy God will hold thy right hand, saying unto thee, Fear not; I will help thee."

Isaiah 54:4—"Fear not; for thou shalt not be ashamed: neither be thou confounded; for thou shalt not be put to shame: for thou shalt forget the shame of thy youth, and shalt not remember the reproach of thy widowhood any more."

Matthew 10:28—"And fear not them which kill the body, but are not able to kill the soul: but rather fear him which is able to destroy both soul and body in hell."

John 14:27—"Peace I leave with you, my peace I give unto you: not as the world giveth, give I unto you. Let not your heart be troubled, neither let it be afraid."

Romans 8:15—"For ye have not received the spirit of bondage again to fear; but ye have received the Spirit of adoption, whereby we cry, Abba, Father."

1 Corinthians 15:58—"Therefore, my beloved brethren, be ye stedfast, unmoveable, always abounding in the work of the Lord, forasmuch as ye know that your labour is not in vain in the Lord."

1 Corinthians 16:13—"Watch ye, stand fast in the faith, quit you like men, be strong."

Ephesians 6:10—"Finally, my brethren, be strong in the Lord, and in the power of his might."

Philippians 1:12—The things which happened unto me have fallen out rather unto the furtherance of the gospel; so that my bonds in Christ are manifest in all the palace, and in all other places; and many of the brethren in the Lord, waxing confident by my bonds, are much more bold to speak the word without fear."

2 Timothy 1:7—"For God hath not given us the spirit of fear; but of power, and of love, and of a sound mind."

Hebrews 13:5, 6—"Let your conversation be without covetousness; and be content with such things as ye have: for he hath said, I will never leave thee, nor forsake thee. So that we may boldly say, The Lord is my helper, and I will not fear what man shall do unto me."

1 Peter 3:14-16—"But and if ye suffer for righteousness' sake, happy are ye: and be not afraid of their terror, neither be troubled; but sanctify the Lord God in your hearts: and be ready always to give an answer to every man that asketh you a reason of the hope that is in you with meekness and fear: having a good conscience; that, whereas they speak evil of you, as of evildoers, they may be ashamed that falsely accuse your good conversation in Christ."

1 John 4:18—"There is no fear in love; but perfect love casteth out fear: because fear hath torment. He that feareth is not made perfect in love."

Chapter 2

Absence of Pain

Lesson: Acknowledge the pain, but stay focused on your work.

I don't expect it to happen in my lifetime. But I didn't realize that its absence could bring such pain.

Studying theology at Washington Adventist University was a positive experience. The Theology Department chair, Bertram Melbourne, not only challenged us in our studies but also encouraged us in our future as pastors. A broad-minded group of young and older men made up the group of fellow students with whom I shared many serious discussions as well as hearty laughs.

Mike Stevenson, a visiting lecturer to one of our senior theology classes, happened to be a local pastor with whom I had attended college. As we chatted after class, I mentioned to him about my upcoming graduation the next summer. He leaned forward, obviously wanting to emphasize a point, looked directly at me, and said in his stately British accent, "Bonita, you must go see my senior pastor, Rob Vandeman, at the Spencerville church. He wants to add a pastor on staff—and he would like to hire a woman."

I might have ignored Mike's advice except that one of my other professors had already said the same thing to me. I thought that maybe God was trying to speak to me through these individuals, so I scheduled an appointment with Pastor Vandeman. During the meeting Pastor Vandeman dialoged with me in a cordial but reserved manner. I explained my situation and pointed out that doing my internship at his church for my last semester might prove beneficial. He remained noncommittal and said, "I'll get back to you." What I didn't know at the time was that after I left his office, he immediately called my department chair to find out more about me. Pastor Vandeman later said to me, "Here I was wondering who or how we would fill this pastoral position, and God sent you right to my office!"

I began my internship in January 1995. The staff consisted of Rob Vandeman, senior pastor; Steve Willsey, associate pastor; and Mike Stevenson, youth pastor. They were a great group of men to work with. Rob was laid-back, but rest assured that you didn't put anything over on him! Everybody loved Steve. Births, weddings, or funerals—Steve was there. And the best word to describe Mike is energetic. Even while we were in college, he had more energy than should be legal!

I told Rob that after I completed my internship, I would appreciate an opportunity to be considered for the full-time pastoral position. Even while an intern, I felt like an integral part of the pastoral team at Spencerville. The only thing that puzzled me at times was that I wasn't included in some board meetings. I didn't know that the reason was that they were talking about me! By February Rob had already started the process of bringing me on staff.

> We do what we do because it is our way of using our God-given creativity to make the world a better place.

My graduation class from college that summer of 1995 consisted of three theology majors: Tony, an Hispanic male; Vernon, a Black male; and me, a White female. We couldn't have been a more politically correct trio if we tried. Tony went on to pastor in Pennsylvania. Vernon went to the seminary to continue his theological education. And I began my pastoral ministry on July 1, 1995, at the Spencerville church—becoming the first full-time female pastor to serve in the Chesapeake Conference.

It's Bigger Than the O Word

I went into pastoral ministry realizing that ordination was not an option for me. I asked the Lord to deliver me from the resentment to which some female pastors had succumbed regarding our church's current stand on ordination. I didn't want to become a bitter woman. I didn't want to become a male-basher. I wanted to focus on ministering to God's people.

You may think it an absurd statement, but I do not believe that ordination is the issue in the dialogue about women in ministry. Frankly, I believe—along with many others in our church—that the current way we conduct ordination in the church is not biblical. The issue in the dialogue about women in ministry is the devaluation of women.[1] I also believe this devaluation of women affects the lives of women in every culture and profession.

Having said that, I find that it doesn't make it any easier to be a female pastor and watch as your male colleagues, with whom you have studied and ministered, are acknowledged by their church as being "called" of God while you are not acknowledged that way. It's similar to the longing that a young girl feels when she's denied the opportunity to play on the school soccer team because of her gender. It's the same yearning any woman feels who has worked hard in whatever vocation God has called her to, only to be unrecognized for her work merely because of her gender.

> A sense of humor is the gift of observing the passing parade and laughing at appropriate moments.

I think I can speak for many women when I say that we don't do what we do for recognition. Sure, having a job helps to pay the bills and to keep food on the table. But deeper than that, we do what we do because it is our way of using our God-given creativity to make the world a better place. Thus, it's difficult for women who have acquired the appropriate education, labored hard in their profession, and sacrificed in other areas of their lives to be denied or overlooked for greater responsibility and service merely because of their gender. It's even more difficult when their church, which they love, perpetuates this injustice.

However, on a spiritual level, we must not allow this to become a battle of *us against them*—women against men. That only serves to strengthen Satan's attempts to build a dividing wall between the genders. He knows the strength that partnership between the genders offers, especially within spiritual leadership. Whether in the personal, professional, or pastoral world, men and women have much to learn from each other. If there is to be a battle, it must be *us*—male and female—against *him*. "For our struggle is not against flesh and blood, but against the rulers, against the authorities, against the powers of this dark world and against the spiritual forces of evil in the heavenly realms" (Eph. 6:12, NIV). Satan would like nothing more than to cripple our church by having us fight among ourselves about the roles of men and women—or any other topic, for that matter. For the sake of God's work, and for the sake of our souls, we must embrace our differences and work together as unified soul winners for Christ.

Most men with whom I have worked have taught me a great deal about life and work. I appreciate their viewpoints. I appreciate their willingness to understand mine. I appreciate those men who allow me to express my frustration with circumstances in which gender prejudice has taken place and who do not feel threatened by my expression of it. I also appreciate their openness to express their frustrations with dealing with gender issues, trusting that I am "man enough" to handle it!

What the World Needs Now

If there is any area in which our world needs reconciliation, it is in the area of gender relations. Ruth Haley Barton's book *Equal to the Task* speaks to this partnership between the genders. As Barton speaks about writing her book, she shares what she believes was her directive:

"I was to let my true voice speak with all of the passion and love and hope I hold in my heart about the possibilities for men and women pulling together. But I was to strengthen the male voice as well and allow men to speak from their hearts the stories, experiences and longings that move in places that are beyond words. I had spent years trying to make sense out of my own journey as a woman; but now I was to listen to the men in my life, not to judge them or convince them or change them but to enter into their experiences in the same way that I had been asking them to enter into mine. . . . We were to speak honestly about what it means to be man and woman, brother and sister. It would be another baby step toward creating a common life, a life that we can all share." [2]

No one gets out of this world unscathed. Women carry wounds, but so do men. While we do not deny or minimize our wounds, I believe we must also seek to acknowledge our brothers' wounds. In our desire to be understood, we must also seek to understand.

Donna[3] was an associate pastor on a multipastor staff. She perceived a wall between herself and a male colleague. There were ministerial opportunities in which they could have collaborated as colleagues, but that didn't happen. Because of her own insecurity, she thought that maybe she had done something wrong and that this was the reason for his lack of respect. She spoke with her senior pastor and asked his opinion as to whether her actions might be causing the problem. He told her, "Donna, when people feel insecure, they don't always handle it the same. You handle it by going inward—wondering if you did something wrong. Others handle it by placing themselves in competition with those around them. That's what [your male colleague] is doing—keeping you at a distance because his insecurity exhibits itself in competing with you."

Donna told me later, "It never crossed my mind that he was feeling insecure and was competing with me. That knowledge really helped me not only to accept myself and my abilities more but to accept him as well."

I know the Lord led me into pastoral ministry. I don't need anyone to prove that to me, although being publicly recognized would be appreciated.[4] But I cannot allow the pain of its absence to allow me to become bitter toward my brothers in Christ or to keep me from what is most important: my ministry to God's people. Its absence would be even more painful.

---

[1] See appendix, "Ordination Is Not the Issue."

[2] Ruth Haley Barton, *Equal to the Task: Men and Women in Partnership* (Downers Grove, Ill.: InterVarsity Press, 1998), p. 14.

[3] Not her real name.

[4] I am thankful for having been given a commissioning ceremony—one that, unfortunately, most of my female colleagues have not received.

Dialogue Questions

1. Why is it important for you to recognize that God has put you where you can do something to build up His kingdom?

2. In what ways do you feel called by God to do what you're doing?

3. What do you think is behind the incessant and pervasive—but often unspoken—attitude in the church that some people are more important than others?

4. How can we, as individuals, encourage other Christian women and men to understand God's call to service in their lives?

Chapter 3

A Time to Laugh

Lesson: Humor is serious business.

The most difficult decision of my day has nothing to do with my professional responsibilities or even crisis situations. Usually I make those decisions with relative ease. The most difficult decision of my day is what to make for dinner. The second most difficult decision, at least when I was a local church pastor, was where to sit in pastors' meetings.

Once every other month the pastors of the Chesapeake Conference met at the conference office to be professionally enriched. The leaders of the Chesapeake Conference were a very dedicated and capable group. Neville Harcombe served as president during most of my tenure, and Rob Vandeman served as ministerial secretary, having left his position as senior pastor at the Spencerville church about six months after he hired me. (Come to think of it, Mike Stevenson also moved elsewhere soon after my arrival—*I didn't realize I had that effect on people!*)

Arriving at the pastors' meetings proved to be an exercise in discretion. As I entered the room, I usually stopped to survey the situation. The other pastors, who were all male, usually sat with an empty seat in between them. (I observed that this was a particularly male habit in these circumstances.) However, that left me in a quandary. I thought, *If the men don't want to sit next to one another, do I really think they want a female colleague to squeeze in next to them?* I really did feel their pain as I walked past some who showed visible signs of discomfort at the thought of my doing just that. Thus, I usually chose to sit near the back of the room where there were several seats vacant in a row.

Neville and Rob supported my role as a pastor. I felt fortunate to be in an environment in which I felt affirmed by my leaders. So when Neville referred to us pastors in these meetings as "you guys," I knew what he meant. I didn't take it personally. "You guys" is a common expression; I use it at times. But I also felt a need to express that it might be nice to hear some inclusive language at times. However, I didn't want to come across heavy-handed in this suggestion. What was I to do?

One day as Neville stood up front speaking to us in his usual collegial tone of voice, he used the expression "you guys," as he often did. Yet it was one of those instances when I knew the time had come. My intuitive thinking and humor kicked in. Although I had not planned it beforehand, I knew what to do. After Neville used "you guys" once again, I casually responded to his question, in the deepest voice I could muster, "Yes, sir!"

Neville stopped talking and looked directly at me. Then he broke into a smile of recognition. *He got it!* He apologized and corrected his course. After that he occasionally slipped, but caught himself most of the time.

My opinion is that many men—as well as many women—use noninclusive language merely because the masculine pronoun is society's default mode. They don't intend to be exclusive. (Some men *do* intend to be exclusive, but that discussion is dealt with in another chapter!) Yet if we can learn to see the humor in some of these situations, learn to laugh at ourselves, and assume the best in others until or unless they prompt you to think otherwise, I believe we will make strides in male–female relations.

Holy Humor

After my tenure as a church pastor, I became an editor at the *Adventist Review* magazine. Our readers often submit comments about articles or topics of interest. One reader contacted me and attempted to convince me that Jesus never laughed. We had a friendly discussion and ultimately agreed to disagree. While I cannot point to a "thus saith the Lord" that Jesus laughed, I can't help wondering, *Would children have been so drawn to Jesus if He was such a somber figure?*

Tom Mullen wrote, "Humorous laughter is a gift God has given humanity. Contrary to popular opinion, the funniest jokes are not made up; they are discovered. A sense of humor is the gift of observing the passing parade and laughing at appropriate moments. Life itself provides the raw material for laughter."[1]

When I speak of laughter, I'm focusing on authentic laughter, the kind that arises from shared life experiences and the naturally humorous circumstances that can result. Jesus used humor to get important points across to His audiences that might have blinded them otherwise. Matthew 23:24 gives us an example. Jesus, talking to the Pharisees and teachers of the law, said, "You blind guides! You strain out a gnat but swallow a camel" (NIV). In the words of *Adventist Review* coordinating editor Steve Chavez, "that's certainly an image worthy of the talents of the folks at Pixar. How do you swallow a camel? Feetfirst? Headfirst? Either way, it's going to be quite a [hilarious] sight."[2]

Proverbs 17:22 says, "A cheerful heart is good medicine, but a crushed spirit dries up the bones" (NIV). Interestingly, the Hebrew word for medicine in that text literally means "healing." In other words, *a cheerful (joyful, glad) heart heals.*

This call to embrace humor doesn't negate the tragic devaluation of women that is present in society and affects not only decisions concerning women in pastoral ministry but also the worth of women in all walks of life, from the workplace to the home.[3] We must take humor seriously. Allowing ourselves to embrace the humor in a situation helps us to acknowledge that we are *all* in need of God's grace and healing. It is by God's grace that we are to minister to one another and to our world. It is through this grace that humor, rightly used, can be a vehicle for others to be able to lower their walls of defense and see the problem more clearly. "Humor reminds us of our fragility, our weakness, our humanity. It teaches us not to take ourselves too seriously. It helps us learn humility."[4] Humor often heals.

Contrary to popular opinion, the funniest humor is not derived at the expense of others. Some people's attempts at humor are poor at best and offensive at worst. I don't think that healing humor can be contrived or thought up. It is derived through the art of observing life and finding the humor inherent within. Sometimes it just sneaks up on you—which can be challenging, especially when you're in a business meeting and are expected to behave professionally and keep a straight face. (My colleague Gary occasionally has to keep me in line. He jokingly shakes his finger at me as if to say, "I know you're about to burst out laughing, Bonita, but now is not the time!")

Almost everyone in my generation remembers the humorist Erma Bombeck. Erma once shared why she was a humor writer: "What I have been doing for 16 years in my column is to put my life in perspective, the frustration of raising children, the loneliness, the pain, and the futility of it all. And it works."[5]

I believe when we as Christian men and women come to where we are able to accept our weaknesses and in humility not take ourselves too seriously, we can diminish the frustration, loneliness, and pain from this wall of gender separation. As Erma has shown us, humor can help us to keep our lives and work in perspective—God's perspective. For aren't we

all merely seeking to live out God's will in the most faithful way possible?
    Live a little. Laugh a little. And remember that when we laugh with one another in the workplace and in the home, we form a bond that can see us through the bumps in the road.

---

[1] Tom Mullen, *Laughing Out Loud* (Richmond, Ind.: Friends United Press, 1989), p. 19.

[2] Stephen Chavez, "Jesus Laughed," *Adventist Review*, June 8, 2006.

[3] See appendix, "Ordination Is Not the Issue."

[4] Cal Samra, *The Joyful Christ* (New York: Harper and Row, 1986), p. 10.

[5] *Ibid.*, p. xii.

Dialogue Questions

1. Of all your friends and acquaintances, whose sense of humor do you enjoy the most? Why?

2. What role does the Holy Spirit play in developing a proper and constructive sense of humor?

3. Can you remember a situation in which a sense of humor diffused a tense situation? Recall it briefly.

4. Can Christians be truly balanced emotionally and spiritually without an appreciation for good and appropriate humor? Explain.

Chapter 4

Didn't You Just Say That?

Lesson: Don't apologize for your opinion.

I used to find comfort in believing that when we get to heaven we won't have to attend committee meetings. Then I read the first chapter of Job. "One day the heavenly beings came to present themselves before the Lord, and Satan also came among them" (verse 6, NRSV). Obviously, since Satan isn't part of the "in" crowd in heaven, this verse isn't discussing a party. It sure sounds like a committee to me. (I hope I've interpreted it wrong.)

I must be fair and say that I think committees can be quite helpful and productive—if led well and governed by certain parameters. I value the wisdom of a larger group when I'm making decisions. I learn a lot from these exchanges. One lesson I've learned is that when a woman chairs a committee, nine times out of 10 its duration is *much* shorter than when a man chairs it. However, one of the lessons I've learned from men in these situations is that they never apologize for their opinion the way we women do. Men often state their opinion as if it's only natural that others will agree with them.

Not all women are regularly exposed to this scenario. Heidi was one of those women. Heidi was a children's ministry leader at my church. She and I sat together one evening at a church board meeting. The topic of discussion was the church building project. Several members expressed their opinions on the matter. Heidi leaned over to me and whispered her thought for a good solution to the problem. I thought it was a great idea. I told her to tell the group.

When the time came, Heidi expressed her opinion, albeit rather timidly. For those who know Heidi, *timid* is not a word people typically use to describe her. But it's interesting how otherwise forthright women turn timid when delivering their opinions in the male-dominated arena of committees. The members appeared to listen to her suggestion and then asked for other feedback.

About 15 minutes later, while we were still working through this topic, a man spoke up. He expressed exactly the same idea as Heidi's; however, he did so more forcefully—and as if nobody else had thought of it before.

"That sounds like it could work," said the board chair.

"Yes, that's great!"

"Let's go with it."

The decision was made. I looked at Heidi. She looked at me. I whispered to her, "Didn't you just say that?" (Heidi read this chapter and commented, "That sure wouldn't happen now!")

Do You Hear What I Hear?

This scenario is not unusual. Men and women use different conversational styles, and unfortunately, a woman's style isn't always heard in the male-dominated arena of committee meetings. I don't think that men, as a rule, intend to ignore a woman's viewpoint. I just can't help wondering if men honestly *hear* women.

Deborah Tannen, professor of linguistics at Georgetown University, addresses men's and women's different conversational styles in her book *Talking From 9 to 5.*[1] Tannen states that women face a special challenge: their conversational style works to deny them the advancement or respect they desire. Often it's not *what you say* but *how you say it* or *who you are*.

Tannen offers several suggestions to women in the workplace about what they can do to ensure that people with varying conversation styles, both men and women, are heard at meetings:

Change our conversation style.

Try being consciously assertive and forceful. Tannen offers a word of caution, however: "This will work for some. But it may be unpleasant for others. . . . And the results will not always be positive."[2] This doesn't have to be a drastic change from your natural style. Even if a woman were to cease using the words "I'm sorry, but . . ." when she shares her thoughts and opinions, that would go a long way toward changing the level of her influence. If you were to intentionally listen to women's conversations, it might surprise you how frequently we apologize for nothing. At times I find myself falling into this habit.

"I'm sorry, but I have to leave early."

"I'm sorry to interrupt, but I have an idea."

"I'm sorry; I won't be able to do the work for you today that you should be doing, but I don't have the guts to tell you it's yours to do!"

As my mother told me: "Your opinion is just as good as anyone else's." (Another lesson: listen to your mother!)

Become skilled at observing group process and notice the role that each group member assumes.

Jerry Lutz, who was my senior pastor at the Spencerville church, is an excellent teacher. I found it very rewarding to work as an intern and associate under his leadership in that he took every opportunity possible to teach me.

Church nominating committees have their challenges, and Spencerville was no exception. However, before we went into one of our meetings in which we had to make a difficult decision concerning a man who had been nominated, Jerry privately informed me about a dynamic taking place in the group.

"Bonita, I want you to watch ———. Notice how she works the room." Later, as I observed the meeting, I was totally unprepared for the manipulation that was taking place before my eyes. This well-educated, articulate woman, like a conductor orchestrating a group of musicians, would call on one person whom she knew would give her the response she wanted, elicit that person's response, then call on the next person who would do this for her. She called on several people throughout the room to build her case. Ultimately she "won." She built her case and turned the tide in the meeting, and unfortunately, a young man paid the price for her manipulation of the process. I learned a lesson about the agenda behind the agenda of a meeting. (Please note that both men and women use manipulation tactics.)

Before a meeting that you will chair, talk privately to each person who will attend. Get everyone's opinions and coordinate everyone's interests.

People are often more willing to share their viewpoints one-on-one than in a group. The Japanese call this practice *nemawashi,* which is an informal process of quietly laying the foundation for some proposed change or project by talking to the people involved and gathering support and feedback. *Nemawashi* means "to go around something." Originally *nemawashi* meant literally digging around the roots of a tree to prepare it for a transplant. If you speak to people ahead of time, as you chair the meeting you can go around the room and invite each member to express his or her thoughts, and that person will likely feel more free and at ease to do so.

My natural tendency is to question and/or apologize for my opinion. I've not totally overcome this tendency; however, a couple of things have helped me reshape it. First, being the only female in my theology classes for most of my educational life as well as the only female in many clergy situations, I've sat quietly and listened through many discussions. I came to realize that others were expressing the thoughts I was having myself. *So why not express them myself?*

Second, I realized that by merely sitting quietly in these situations, I removed my voice from the discussions. I began to believe that my opinion mattered, and I learned to jump into the discussions feetfirst. Often the only way to be heard in a male-dominated environment is to jump in when an opening presents itself! However, I have to recalibrate when I'm in a group of women, or I can unintentionally dominate the conversation.

> If you were to intentionally listen to women's conversations, it might surprise you how frequently we apologize for nothing.

One Voice

I recently took my mother shopping. While in a department store, I asked a teenage girl for directions to the fitting room. After she directed me, she handed me an index card that had been ripped in half. On it were these handwritten words: "Dear Reader, you are wonderful, amazing, so very precious, *beautiful*, and you are *loved*! Never let *anyone* tell you otherwise! You have a voice—use it. *One Voice* saves lives—one voice saved mine. Sincerely, Anonymous."

You have a voice. One voice. Your voice matters. Your voice can have a more far-reaching effect on life than you realize. Don't apologize for your opinion. *The world* would do well to listen to the voices of women and address the devaluation that has been present in society for millennia.[3] *God's people* would do well to hear the voices of women and acknowledge the women who make up almost 70 percent of the church's membership. *Men* need to embrace women's voices and partner with their female counterparts to accomplish more effectively the work we have been given. Women served within Jesus' inner circle of followers. Paul labored side by side with women in spreading the gospel.[4] Both Jesus and Paul lived and taught the value that the gospel places on women.

How can you learn to use your voice more?

1. **Start small.** In your circle of friends, where it's "safe," begin to share your opinions. As you build more confidence, you can branch out into sharing at work, church, and other arenas.

2. **Ask questions.** This is a good way to help you understand what others are basing their opinions on, but it can also encourage others to ask you for your opinion.

3. **Read.** As you become more versed on various topics, you will have more to contribute to the conversation. Scanning the headlines of online news sites helps persons to stay connected to relevant discussion topics. Even if you don't know much about a topic, these practices can at least help you to know what questions to ask.

I don't feel the need to jump into every conversation. There are times that I just sit back and listen to the dialogue. But now when I choose to listen, I feel as though I have made the choice to be silent.

Even though I no longer reflexively apologize for my opinion, I still hope there aren't any committees in heaven. Depending on who's running them, they could go on *forever.*

---

[1] Visit http://www9.georgetown.edu/faculty/tannend/ for a listing of all of Deborah Tannen's books.

[2] Deborah Tannen, *Talking From 9 to 5* (New York: William Morrow, 1994), p. 304.

[3] See appendix, "Ordination Is Not the Issue."

[4] See Mark 15:40, 41; Luke 24:22; 1 Corinthians 16; and 3 John as a few examples.

Dialogue Questions

1. Most of us have experienced small groups and committees. What about them do you like? What do you dislike?

2. In a small group or committee, when do you feel most comfortable speaking up? When do you feel most inhibited?

3. In addition to the words spoken, what other clues should you look for during a meeting?

4. How would your small group or committee be different if Jesus were leading the meeting?

Chapter 5

Half Past Twice

Lesson: Acknowledging your needs reveals strength, not weakness.

Although I fought hard against the idea that pastors must be perfect, it wasn't difficult for me to fall into the trap of *trying* to be perfect.

Sabbath mornings are the climax of a pastor's week. Often that's the primary time we connect with most of our church members. As I fluttered through the foyer and hallways, trying to see as many people as possible, I often ran into Teofilo Ferrera (not literally, of course).

Teofilo, a pastor himself, worked at the church's world headquarters. He possessed a calm and thoughtful way about him. I don't remember when he started asking me pointed questions, but I am forever grateful he did.

One Sabbath morning Teofilo greeted me in the hallway and asked, "Bonita, how are you?"

I answered with the usual "I'm fine, Teofilo. How are you?"

He looked at me with his piercing eyes and asked me again in a slow, intentional voice, emphasizing the words in the question, "No, Bonita, *how . . . are . . . you?*"

I sensed the usual shallow answer wasn't going to cut it with him. When I realized that he held an honest concern about *me* and that he wasn't just trying to make small talk, I felt safe to sincerely respond. "I'm tired," I said. Of course, this wasn't news to him. He had figured it out long before I admitted it.

I shared with Teofilo that while I loved my work and my church members, trying to balance work and home and time with my husband—life—was taking it out of me. He then made a statement that took me by surprise: "Bonita, you *do* realize that as a female pastor you have to work twice as hard to be half as good."

I've always tried hard not to succumb to the "us-against-them" mentality in ministry. Thus, if this comment had come from a woman I might have discounted it as biased, and I probably would not have allowed myself to accept it. But hearing it from a man gave me "permission" to ponder its significance. Something deep within me began responding to his statement. I had not consciously acknowledged this reality, but my soul knew it.

> Hearing it from a man gave me "permission" to ponder its significance.

Yes, I knew that my own insecurities contributed to my unrealistic expectations of myself. I spent a lot of emotional energy trying to measure up to an unspoken, unidentifiable standard that could never quite be reached. However, Teofilo's words forced me to realize that these unrealistic expectations were also present outside of my emotional makeup.

Working Harder

The notion that a woman needs to work twice as hard to be half as good is not unique to gospel ministry. One woman who is an environmental engineer says this of her career environment: "There aren't many women working in this field in general, and it is even rarer to encounter a female Ph.D. I've actually had clients question my expertise because of my gender and appearance—some outright telling me that they would feel more comfortable talking to one of my male employees, even knowing that they were less experienced and answered to me."[1]

What often happens when women encounter such situations is that they work harder to make up for this perception that they are not quite as good as their male counterparts. Working harder is not a bad thing. But when we work harder and harder, denying our own legitimate needs because we think that if we let down our guard we won't "measure up," everyone loses.

By nature women are nurturers. Of course, there are exceptions to this rule. But, generally speaking, women do a better job of nurturing than men do. Unfortunately, we often work so hard at taking care of everyone around us that we neglect our own legitimate needs. This happens not only in the home but in the office as well. "I can't take a vacation. What would my boss do without me?" "I know it's not my job to do, but I don't want to burden my colleague, even though it's his/her job."

I am a peacekeeper by nature. I am also a people pleaser. Not a good combination. I have allowed myself to spend too much of my life dealing with the negative emotions that arise from my trying to meet the needs of everyone around me—except mine. Society—parents, school, church, and the media—succeeds at reinforcing the message to women that their needs are unimportant and that their main role in the home and in the workplace is to take care of the needs of everyone around them. Of course, as Christians we are to love and to serve others. And women hold a unique nurturing role within the home. But the Lord has had to work in my life to strip me of the false humility that arises from neglecting my needs for the sake of others' needs.

This is not an essay on how to become self-centered! However, it is a call for women to acknowledge their own needs so that they can possess the physical, spiritual, and emotional strength to reach out to and nurture those around them. It is a reminder that acknowledging one's needs personally, professionally, or pastorally is not self-centered or weak. It is a challenge for us women to learn a lesson from many of our male counterparts on how to respect ourselves and take time to rejuvenate and refresh our bodies and minds.

In John 17 we find the last prayer that Jesus prayed with His disciples before He was arrested and sentenced to death on the cross. This prayer can be divided into three parts: Jesus praying for Himself, for His disciples, and for us. But notice that He begins His prayer *by praying for Himself.* Was Jesus selfish by praying first for Himself? Of course not. It's the same principle that we find when airlines tell us to place the oxygen mask on ourselves before we try to place it on someone else: *we cannot help someone else if we aren't in a position to help them.* Airlines know that we cannot help someone else breathe if we ourselves can't breathe. Jesus knew He needed His Father's blessing before He could accomplish the task of saving the world. I hope we, as women, will learn that we cannot nurture others if we have nothing physically, emotionally, or spiritually to draw from in ourselves.

How to Ask for Our Needs to Be Met

Asking for our needs to be met is not the same as *demanding* that they be met. Asking for our needs to be met is an example of assertive behavior, which strong leaders tend to exhibit. Assertive behavior respects self while also respecting the other person. Assertive behavior is not aggressive behavior. Aggressive behavior moves against others. And at the other extreme, passive behavior moves against self.[2]

For example, if a work associate makes an unreasonable request of me, a passive response would be for me to fill the request but feel helpless and manipulated, or to "forget" or procrastinate. An aggressive response would be for me to refuse the request with offensive or guilt-inducing words such as, "You've violated my rights! How dare you! Don't you know I'm already overloaded with work?" An assertive response (one that respects self and others) would be either to refuse the request respectfully or to negotiate the request: "You know, John, helping you with that project is not going to work for me." Maybe even add, "Let me give you the name of someone who might be able to help you." Or: "You know, John, Tuesday doesn't work for me to help you with that project, but I have an hour on Thursday. Would that be helpful?" It's also helpful to respond with "Let me think about it. I'll give you an answer later this afternoon." That gives you time to think about an appropriate response if you're caught off guard.[3]

Unfortunately, a colleague or family member may not always respond well when we ask for something that will meet our needs. Even the request for some change in a particular situation can make them feel threatened. Still others just don't want to change—even though the change may be necessary in order for your needs to be met. When this happens, relationships become strained. That can be difficult to accept, especially when the relationships affected are important ones. But the cost of a strained relationship with someone is much lower than the cost to yourself, your health—and sometimes even your life—when you don't ask for your needs to be met.

Nighty-Night

Steve was my pastoral colleague. One of the things I admire about Steve is his ability to remember names. Even the names of those people who attended our church once—and came back six months later—came to his mind quickly. Unfortunately, I'm one of those people who can forget a person's name before the conversation ends! Another thing I admire about Steve is his strength in acknowledging his own needs, especially at evening church board meetings.

These meetings are infamous for running late. An item that should take five minutes to discuss and resolve can take an hour. Ideally, 7:00 board meetings should be done by 8:30 p.m. But life isn't always ideal. Often, we go past 8:30 p.m. and are nowhere near the end of the agenda. I threatened several times to post a quotation of Ellen White stating that no productive work gets accomplished late into the night, which by my clock was after 9:00 p.m.[4] But I'm a wimp. I never followed through on that. On the other hand, Steve never threatened to do anything. He just did it. By 8:45 p.m. or so, Steve, after having put in a full day's work, would stand up from his seat, look around, and say, "It's almost my bedtime. Have a good evening." And he would leave. *Go, Steve!*

I still haven't learned that lesson. I'm working on it, though.

At least now I can admit it.

---

[1] See "'Women Have to Work Twice as Hard to Be Considered Half as Worthy': True or False?" Sodahead: Opinions . . . Everybody's Got One, www.sodahead.com/business/women-have-to-work-twice-as-hard-to-be-considered-half-as-worthy-true-or-false/question-476547/ (accessed Jan. 26, 2013).

[2] Ruth N. Koch and Kenneth C. Haugk, *Speaking the Truth in Love: How to Be an Assertive Christian* (St. Louis: Stephen Ministries, 1992), p. 20.

[3] See Koch and Haugk's *Speaking the Truth in Love* for an assertiveness inventory quiz to discover your assertiveness quotient.

[4] Ellen G. White, *Testimonies for the Church* (Mountain View, Calif.: Pacific Press Pub. Assn., 1948), vol. 7, p. 256. It doesn't state a specific time limit, but it does give the principle of not having meetings be prolonged into the night.

Dialogue Questions

1. What does Christ's promise "Come unto me . . . and I will give you rest" (Matt. 11:28) mean to you?

2. What negative results come from trying to meet unrealistic expectations? What are the physical and emotional prices we pay?

3. How often should a person evaluate the responsibilities and expectations others impose on them to see if they're still valid? Once a year? Once a month? Once a week?

4. What work, church, or family responsibility would you drop in a heartbeat if you could? Why can't you?

Chapter 6

Standing Still for Justice

Lesson: Allow others to "fight" for you.

When the Nazis came for the Communists,
I did not speak out,
As I was not a Communist.
When they locked up the social democrats,
I did not speak out,
As I was not a social democrat.
When they came for the trade unionists,
I did not speak out,
As I was not a trade unionist.
When they came for the Jews,
I did not speak out,
As I was not a Jew.
When they came for me,
there was no one left to speak out.*

This popular poem is attributed to Martin Niemöller (1892-1984), and it's about the inactivity of German intellectuals following the Nazi rise to power. I'm sure most of us have seen variations wherein people have replaced these groups with others they believe to be in need of advocacy. For example, "They came for the homeless, and I did not speak out . . ."; "They came for the children . . ." This poem serves to remind all of us of the responsibility we carry to speak out against injustices done to those around us—to use our voices on behalf of those who have no voice. It elicits in us a courage and boldness to stand for justice. And it serves to confront us with the reality that if we do not advocate for others in need, no one will be present to advocate for us when we are in need.

Have we considered our spiritual responsibility of allowing others to advocate for *us*? It's not always easy for us to receive from others. Take Christmas or birthdays, for example. When someone gives you a gift and you didn't buy him or her one, what do you do? You go out and buy that person a gift, even though you had not planned to buy one! Why? Accepting a gift without trying to repay the giver places us in a position of seeming indebtedness and ungratefulness. To repay keeps us on equal footing.

It takes humility to accept another's advocacy for us rather than to "fight" for ourselves. At least when we are fighting, we feel as if we're doing something about the situation. But think about it. Standing still and allowing others to advocate for us is not a passive stance; it's an act of faith.

The Singing Army

In the mid-ninth century B.C. messengers delivered word to King Jehoshaphat that a great multitude was coming against him from the neighboring country of Edom. The king was frightened, which wasn't unusual. Fear underlies most power struggles. Jehoshaphat could have yelled back, "Oh yeah, well, my army's bigger than your army! We'll see who comes out ahead." However, he didn't. He took his fear to the Lord. He called the people together throughout the kingdom and sought the Lord through prayer and fasting. He ended a lengthy corporate prayer with these words: "We are powerless against this great multitude that is coming against us. We do not know what to do, but our eyes are on you" (2 Chron. 20:12, NRSV).

But here's the kicker. God answered Jehoshaphat's prayer through one of His prophets, who delivers God's message: "Do not fear or be dismayed at this great multitude; for the battle is not yours but God's. . . . This battle is not for you to fight; take your position, stand still, and see the victory of the Lord on your behalf" (verses 15-17).

The next morning they went out to meet the army. But instead of carrying weapons with which to fight, the "Yahweh Temple Choir" sang praises to God! While they were singing, God set an ambush against their enemies—the Ammonites, Moabites, and Meunites. The first two groups attacked the third group. After they finished that job, the Ammonites and Moabites turned on each other and destroyed each other. No one survived.

Don't think it was easy for the Israelites to stand still. Would you be skipping along and humming a tune while an army was ready to destroy you? I imagine it took every ounce of self-discipline and faith in God's power to wait on Him. What I believe this did for Jehoshaphat and his army was to remind them *whose* army they were in and that they did not—and should not—seek to control every situation; the lesson applies to us as well. When we do try to always be in control, we can quite easily fall into the resulting bitterness and resentment.

At different times in my life I have found myself in situations in which I realized it was not wise or best for me to "fight" the battle. One situation I think of involved the parsonage allowance that every clergyperson is entitled to in the United States. Mine was being withheld. I was assured time and again that it was coming; some "administrative technicalities had to be worked out." However, I knew of no male pastors who were experiencing this difficulty.

After several attempts to rectify the situation, I asked two male colleagues to advocate for me. They willingly agreed. No "war," no fuss, just two persons who held more power than I did, who would go to bat for me and were willing to ask the hard questions on my behalf. It wasn't easy for me to "sit still" and wait. Singing more praise songs might have helped! Ultimately, though, the situation was rectified. But I firmly believe that had these godly men not intervened, it might have taken much longer, and it would have adversely affected me spiritually—and maybe even physically. I thank God that others were willing to advocate for me.

> Standing still and allowing others to advocate for us is not a passive stance; it's an act of faith.

There are times we must wait upon the Lord and seek the assistance of others to fight for us, but there are times we need to become the "warrior" in a battle, times we must don our armor and step into the line of fire and speak up. If inappropriate or abusive physical or verbal treatment is taking place, we must make a choice to seek help and then stand up for ourselves and make a change.

And remember: men also experience abuse—to a much smaller degree, but they do nonetheless. One instance that speaks to this came about when I left business cards in the restrooms at my workplace that offered help to people who were experiencing abuse. Typically, I placed them only in the women's restroom. However, I placed some in the men's restrooms as well. Sometime later a man came to my office and thanked me for doing so. He then shared with me how his former wife used to abuse him physically, which included hitting him as well as cornering him with a large knife in her hand. He was grateful we were also acknowledging men's silent suffering.

In the workplace—and even in a church or parachurch environment—inappropriate or abusive treatment can happen, including sabotage, bullying, putdowns, blaming, or outright physical harm to oneself or to one's property. In these situations I encourage you to find someone outside of the situation to support you in the decisions you must make. You can also search online for "workplace harassment," "workplace violence," and other phrases to find excellent resources by reputable organizations.

In circumstances that don't include inappropriate or abusive treatment you can use these situations as opportunities to allow others to fight for you and thus protect you from the spiritual damage that can result from always trying to fight for yourself.

A Bitter Prayer

When I first began to realize that the Lord wanted me to go into pastoral ministry, my first response—after I got over the initial feeling of terror—was "Lord, I don't want to become a bitter woman." Daily I continue to pray that prayer. Why? Is it because female pastors are bitter, angry women trying to push themselves into ministry? No. I pray that prayer because I know the challenges that women face in spiritual and corporate leadership positions. I pray that prayer because I know women who have become angry and bitter from the injustices they have experienced in the workplace. In addition, I pray that prayer because if I don't, I could easily become one of those bitter women. I could become embroiled in the "battle" against the injustice of a system that penalizes a person because of their gender, instead of recognizing that both male and female are made in the image of God, who wills to speak to us through both genders. But injustice in the workplace is not the only battle women face. They experience battles regarding their work being taken seriously. They experience battles regarding equal pay for equal work. And they experience the even more serious battle for their *lives* in countries in which women have no or very few rights. Often these women have no voice—not because they are incapable, but because they hold no power.

It is because of all these battles that we must learn not only to *stand* for justice and speak up for others who have no voice but also to be willing to *stand still* for justice when necessary and allow others to speak for us when *we* have no voice.

Remember the poem by Niemöller and the line "When they came for me . . ."

Will you have the courage to *stand still* and watch the victory of the Lord on your behalf?

---

* Niemöller wrote several versions of this poem, the first in 1946. In 1971 Niemöller said in an interview that he preferred the version I have quoted. See "Martin Niemöller," Wikiquote, http://en.wikiquote.org/wiki/Martin_Niemöller.

Dialogue Questions

1. Who are the vulnerable "others" in your life? List at least 10.

2. What makes us prone to define "others" in terms of how they are different from us? Why can that be dangerous?

3. What primary emotions come to the forefront when you feel threatened? What Bible stories or texts speak to these responses either positively or negatively?

4. Is warfare in the Christian life inevitable? If so, what are our primary weapons? Who is our primary "enemy"?

Chapter 7

Still a Lady[1]

Lesson: Advocating for equality does not mean denying your gender identity.

I don't mind being the only female in a group of male colleagues. What I do mind is being asked to deny my gender identity.

After a long morning of lectures, my seminary class and our professor would search out the nearest restaurant for a bite to eat.[2] This particular day we found a nice Italian eatery close to our meeting location. It was springtime, so we sat outdoors around a large round table and chatted about our classwork, families, and whatever else we happened to think about.

When it came time to order, the server approached our table and asked who was ready to order first. One of my classmates turned to me, smiled, and cordially said, "Ladies first." Before I could respond, another classmate turned to me and asked in a sarcastic tone, "But what about this egalitarian stuff?"

At this point everyone's gaze turned to me. H'mmm. How was I going to respond? Would I tear his eyes out? (Just kidding!) Would I falter and fumble? Would I pretend I didn't hear him? After thinking for a moment—and praying for wisdom—I smiled and responded, "Yes, we are all equal. But I'm *still* a lady."

What I find disconcerting in our society is the misguided notion that in order to achieve equality between the genders, we must blur the lines between male and female. Have you ever noticed how sometimes it is difficult to tell a man and a woman apart from each other? Women do not have to wear frou-frou-frilly clothing (thank the Lord!) to be viewed as female, but they also don't have to dress exactly like men. Women are not weaklings who cannot open doors for themselves, but there is nothing wrong with a man holding a door for a woman and her acknowledging his kind gesture. What is it that makes both men and women think that in order to be equal, they must deny that there are any differences between them?

Extreme Makeover

Two extremes exist in this discussion, and both exemplify a typical human tendency toward imbalance. One extreme view denies the unique qualities of being a female and tries to morph the genders together—physically as well as emotionally. Besides pressuring women to look and dress the same as men, often we refuse women the privilege of expressing themselves congruent with their gender, which places them in a no-win situation.

For example, in general, women in the workplace tend to view the *relationship* as more important than the *rules*. I've observed that when a woman does this, she's considered a "soft touch." Yet if that same woman attempts to view the *task* as of utmost importance (congruent with her male counterparts' tendencies), she's more often than not accused of being a female dog. We call this predicament a catch-22. However, if a man operates from the vantage point of *relationships*, he's considered "a gentle man." And if he is a type A, tasked-oriented individual, he's considered "a strong leader."

The other extreme is the view that honors the differences between the genders but relegates them to certain roles that are "permissible" for that gender. This extreme postulates that women do indeed have unique qualities but that these should be exercised only in "womanly work," such as running a home, raising children, and doing deaconess duties at church. If they want to exercise their talents and/or giftedness outside of the home, they could be nurses or pastors' wives, maybe even elementary school teachers. Some in this camp suggest that women are intellectually inferior to men.

What is it that makes both men and women think that in order to be equal, they must deny that there are any differences between them?

Countless stories abound of women who dreamed of and felt called to be pastors, doctors, or other professionals but who were discouraged or dissuaded because of these biases to their gender. I listened to one story recently of a woman who had dreamed of becoming a pastor. She obtained her theological education yet was never given the opportunity to pastor. Even after several decades, the pain is still evident in her face and voice when she shares it.

God indeed made women different from men. (My husband and I really like it that way.) Yet how do we embrace our differences? How do we honor what God created women and men to be without denying either gender their freedom as children of God? What would our workplaces, churches, and homes look like if we were to respect our gender differences more fully?

We would communicate

If men and women were to respect their gender differences more fully, they would use their gender strengths to communicate—without apology. Accomplishing this task takes humility on both sides. It takes humility for men to accept that there is another equally valid way of thinking, as well as another equally valid way of relating to a situation. On the flip side, it takes humility for women to accept that not all men are out to get them. Women need to be willing to put aside their defensiveness and learn from their male counterparts.

We would create balance

If men and women were to respect their gender differences more fully, they would use their gender strengths to create balance. There is a time for relationships to prevail, and there is a time for rules to prevail. The challenge is to be willing to acknowledge that one way is not superior to the other—just different. We must work as a team to use our strengths to resolve any imbalances that might come about. Actually, I've been in all-female work situations, and I pushed for men to be included because I believed that an all-female staff was unbalanced. As much as I love my gender, in high school I chose to play on a co-ed softball team rather than an all-female team because having both genders made for a balanced team. But it must go both directions.

God created humankind in His image, after His likeness; male and female He created *them* (see Gen. 1:27). Seeking to represent God through only one gender is a distortion and misrepresentation of God's image.

We would accept our differences

If men and women were to respect their gender differences more fully, they would do so without trying to fashion the other in their own image. In the corporate world—secular and religious—it's a known fact that if leaders do not consciously select colleagues and support staff who complement and counterbalance their strengths and weaknesses, they will choose those who naturally reflect themselves, creating an imbalance. Insecure people often choose mirror images of themselves.

My departmental director, Jonathan Kuntaraf, is an excellent example of a secure leader. Jonathan is one of the most godly, secure leaders I know (right up there with former *Adventist Review* editor William Johnsson). While he amazes our staff with his insight into how the organization runs, he works his way through its roadblocks and barriers with grace and Christian courtesy. He listens to his staff even when we disagree with him. On more than one occasion he has changed his course of action because of our input. He's one of the few leaders I've observed who's willing to share his or her "power" in order to develop others' talents and gifts—male and female alike. Working under his leadership is an affirming experience.

What an opportunity men and women have to embrace this principle and to lead from a vantage point of shared strengths and weaknesses!

After my response that day in the restaurant, my other classmates exclaimed, "Touché!" and urged me to order first. I considered it a victory of sorts, since I didn't resort to my natural tendency to offer a sarcastic rebuttal. Neither did I wilt and say, "You're right. If we're going to be egalitarian, we'll have to play by your rules"—which isn't egalitarian at all. I responded kindly but firmly.

Conduct befitting a lady.

---

[1] I realize the different connotations for *lady*. However, to be truthful to the content of the original discussion, I've chosen to use it for this chapter.

[2] I completed my graduate studies through an off-campus program with Andrews University. Our cohort would meet several times a year at a different location throughout North America for intensive classwork.

Dialogue Questions

1. Are there limits to equality of the genders? If so, what are they? If not, why not?

2. Do double standards exist between the genders? If so, what are some you've observed?

3. In gender equality, are stereotypes the fundamental issue, or is it freedom? Explain.

4. How does contemporary society make it easier or harder to live God's ideal in gender equality?

Chapter 8

You've Got to Start Somewhere

Lesson: Be willing to be the token female.

Many women resist being the token female. However, I've found that if we embrace this role, we can do much to reveal the true worth of the female presence.

I had pastored at my church for almost seven years when I accepted the invitation from William Johnsson to be an assistant editor at the *Adventist Review*. I gave a two-month notice to allow ample time to say my goodbyes. Often members asked me why I had chosen to "leave ministry" to work at the *Adventist Review*. I assured them I was not leaving ministry; I was merely fulfilling my pastoral calling through another venue: the written word.

I loved my time in a church setting. I felt appreciative of the opportunity and privilege to walk alongside my church members in many of life's journeys. Regardless, I would now be able to give my writer's heart and my pastor's heart equal focus in order to nurture God's people worldwide.

As I sat in my church office one day, preparing it for the incoming pastor's use—cleaning out files, packing up mementos, looking out my window at the horse farm, and enjoying the view of the dogwood tree that kept me company each spring—Marie-Jo walked in. She is a soft-spoken French woman who served with me on our women's ministry team. Marie-Jo came to give me a personal farewell. As she stood leaning against my office doorway, she said with her beautiful French accent, "Bonita, I want you to know that when you arrived here at our church, I was against women in ministry. But after having worked with you and seeing you minister, I now support women in ministry." I'm not sure she realized that in her simple goodbye she gave me a never-to-be-forgotten gift.

The Power of Modeling

While my pastoral role was not necessarily a token female role, it speaks volumes to this very point. If women are willing to be the only female presence in a male-dominated arena and seek to understand as well as be understood, I believe their role modeling will do much to break down gender barriers. In the church I don't think most people hold on to theological objections about females in spiritual leadership roles. Much of the problem is that they've never *experienced* the ministry of a female. Certainly, I do not believe that Marie-Jo arrived at her conclusion by merely reading an article in support of women in ministry or by debating the topic. The concept of women in ministry had to become flesh and dwell with her.

Whether it's ministry, education, business, or medicine, in a typically male-dominated environment it often takes the willingness of a woman to be a token female in order for people's views in that environment to begin to expand.

Making a Difference

With any work, it's difficult to know whether you're making a difference in the lives of others. You just do what you believe is right, hoping that somehow you're not the only one changing in the process. In order to make strides in the advancement of women in roles that have historically been filled by men, women must be willing to be the only female presence. Our presence on a committee or in a position may happen merely because someone thought, *We should have a woman in that role.* Frankly, its importance may be diminished in some people's view because "it's only a woman" sitting there. This doesn't mean that we've allowed ourselves to be devalued or demeaned. It means we set aside our pride and realize that this situation can evolve into the opportunity to show how invaluable women's skills, insights, and intelligence can be to a committee, business, hospital, school, or congregation.

Jerry Lutz, my former senior pastor, had never worked with a female associate before coming to the Spencerville church. Below are his thoughts regarding the experience:

"Personal experience has taught me the value and importance of women in ministry during the past 14 years of my 32 years of pastoral ministry. In the interview for my present position, the conference president described for me the makeup of the staff of the Spencerville church. He then very

> The concept of women in ministry had to become real to her.

cautiously asked, 'Would you have a problem with having a woman as an associate pastor?'

"Without hesitation I responded, 'Absolutely not.' In fact, I remember immediately thinking of the advantage of having someone on the team who would have the 'inside edge' when it came to ministering to roughly half of the members of the congregation. But I was very wrong about that, as time would tell. For the past 14 years the *entire* congregation has been blessed by the succession of three women associate pastors—Bonita being the first. I am not alone in this opinion. The evidence is quite convincing, as seen in the changed lives of those to whom they have ministered.

"The women pastors with whom I have served have been able to minister to some whom I know would not be comfortable working with a male pastor. And it works the other way, too. There are times and circumstances in which it is either ill-advised or just plain inappropriate for a male pastor to try to minister to a female parishioner. While we would all like to think that everyone to whom we minister is completely trustworthy and honorable, sadly, history teaches otherwise. Thus, there have been many occasions on which I have been very thankful to be able to refer certain matters to a female pastor.

"Until becoming the senior pastor of the Spencerville Adventist Church, I didn't know what I was missing, having never served before with a woman on a pastoral staff. Unfortunately, the churches in which I had previously pastored didn't know what they were missing either!"

Reducing the Pressure

I live and work alongside some very intelligent, articulate Christian women: administrators, educators, pastors, doctors, editors, and entrepreneurs. Most of them are the only females in an otherwise male-dominated environment, yet they operate with grace and skill. However, women can feel a lot of pressure being the only woman in an otherwise all-male environment. We can feel as if we've got to prove ourselves. In a sense, we do. But I also think that there are a few things we can recognize and do to alleviate some of this pressure.

Imperfection does not equal failure

Remember that the cause of women will not fail if we are not perfect. Women put a lot of pressure on themselves. I know. I've been there and done that—*and* bought the T-shirt! Many women with whom I have counseled have also felt the pressure. However, the inclusion of women in otherwise male-dominated circles isn't dependent on our perfection. I think it's going to be dependent on the Holy Spirit working in the lives of men and women to realize that God's image is not complete or fully represented without the presence of both male and female—especially within the body of Christ. If you offend someone or say something you wish you hadn't said, apologize to the person, *forgive yourself*, and move on!

Learn from your male colleagues

Remember that you can learn much from your male colleagues. Yeah, I know, this one's challenging. While we want to be open to learning, we should be confident in our own abilities. I think the right balance is to be open to learning without falling into the trap of feeling as if we cannot do anything without men. What I mean is that we need to understand the difference between depending on other people ("Thank you, Joe, for visiting Mrs. Smith while I was away; I appreciated your assistance") and being personally dependent on them ("Joe, I just couldn't do my work without you"). We need to learn interdependence.

Having said that, I encourage you to learn to laugh at yourself—and your gender. One time I was the featured speaker at a weekend retreat for college students. After just finishing a Sabbath afternoon walk through the woods—in the rain—we arrived back at the meeting lodge, and the coordinator asked me, "So can we count on you to begin your talk in five minutes?" Fortunately, I had learned to embrace our differences enough by then to say, "You must remember whom you're speaking with—a *female* speaker who has just returned from a walk in the rain and whose hair is a mess! Give me 10 minutes, and I'll be there!" We all had a good laugh. Even more important, it took nothing away from my impact on them as a thought leader. We experienced a powerful time together in our meetings.

When we can view our gender realistically and humbly (neither more *nor less* than what we are), I think many gender walls will be broken down.

Acknowledge your needs

Remember that acknowledging your needs reveals strength—not weakness. This is a difficult one for us as women. We're used to being the caregivers. We're used to taking care of everyone else's needs. We're used to being on the defensive. I must qualify this last comment by saying that unfortunately, many times we've been coerced into this defensive stance.

Defending oneself, after all, is a natural response when someone acts in an aggressive manner. Sadly, many women find themselves in these situations.* However, if we can learn that acknowledging our needs does not make us weak, then the defensiveness and pressure to be perfect will lessen. The strongest men and women I know are those who recognize their limitations.

Being the token female isn't always the most comfortable position to be in. But it has the potential to make a difference in a situation or in a group that otherwise would not have benefited from a female presence. We've got to start somewhere.

---

* The book that has helped me the most in learning how to acknowledge my needs in a godly and assertive manner is Ruth Koch and Kenneth Haugk's *Speaking the Truth in Love*.

Dialogue Questions

1. Who have been your most influential role models? Mention two: one male, one female. How were their influences different? How were they similar?

2. Give three examples from the past about stereotypes and prejudices that had to be overcome. Give three examples from the present that still need to be overcome.

3. Is it easier to live up to the expectations of others than it is to live up to our own expectations? Why or why not?

4. What is the difference between self-confidence and arrogance? How does self-confidence help us carry out our responsibilities?

Chapter 9

You've Got Mail

Lesson: It's not about you.

I love getting letters—even one from a magazine reader who thinks I should resign.

My love of the mailbox began in boarding academy. Long before T-Mobile, texting, and Twitter, snail mail was the primary mode of communication. There were no cell phones, Internet, or friends-and-family telephone rates. Each day I walked down the steps from my dormitory room, meandered past the mailboxes in the dormitory lobby, and looked longingly into the small peephole to see if I had received a coveted letter from home. This connection held me until I made my weekly call home.

When I arrived at the *Adventist Review*, my love of the mailbox continued. Now my anticipation expanded to receiving letters from our readers. Did they like a particular issue? Did they think my editorial stank? Did they have an idea for an article?

When I received my first letter from a reader, I eagerly opened it to see what types of letters readers actually send editors. The man obviously had read my first editorial. His letter read:

"Dear Sister Shields,

"You may be a pastor in your own eyes, but you most certainly are not in the eyes of God, since the Bible clearly reserves the role of elder/pastor to men only. For you to present yourself as a pastor in the face of this evidence and contrary to the decisions of several General Conference sessions is rebellious and well-nigh blasphemous. This obvious lack of spiritual discernment makes you wholly unqualified to be writing articles as spiritual food for God's remnant people. Please resign immediately."

I sat and pondered his words—for about five minutes. OK, 10 minutes. I couldn't help respecting the man for at least signing his name. But I didn't need to mull over his letter, because I realized that his objections were not about me. You may argue, "Of course they were about you!" But I disagree. Yes, this brother obviously had a problem with my calling myself a pastor. But that's *his* problem. That's his problem with *every* female pastor. And that's his problem that he must work out with the Lord. My task was and is to live out my calling as a shepherd of God's people—until He tells me otherwise. (Note: His comment about my going against GC session decisions was factually incorrect.)

Thinking It Doesn't Make It So

I've not always understood or embraced this concept of allowing others to own their own problems. In my early 20s I went to see the chaplain at my place of employment because I couldn't convince a (former) friend of mine that she was wrong in her condemning opinion of me. I experienced great distress over this. Yet I remember the chaplain's words as if he had spoken them yesterday: "Bonita, just because someone thinks something about you, that doesn't make it true."

How liberating! How often have I allowed someone else's problem to become my problem. I would take people's biases and opinions personally instead of seeing them for what they were: *their* biases and opinions. I now understand better who I am in Christ and can allow others their opinions—even if I don't agree with them and even if they involve me. As one woman told me: "Others' opinions of me are none of my business!"

Are there situations in your life, congregation, or workplace in which you feel as if "they" are "out to get you"? Quite honestly, people don't think about us as much as we think they do. For example, when you walk into a room and those present stop talking, your first thought is most likely, *Oh, they must have been talking about me.* I understand. I too have had that thought before. But now when that happens, I tell myself, *Bonita, just because they stopped talking when you arrived doesn't mean they were talking about you. They obviously were talking about something private. And even if they were talking about you, I guess there's one thing worse than people talking about you and that's people not talking about you!*

More Than Gender

When difficulties arise in the workplace, there are times that it *is* about us. And it's not always a bias or gender issue.

Kathleen is a woman who got along well with her boss at the beginning, but after a few months she began to feel overlooked and ignored. Her main task involved helping her boss choose projects for their foundation to support, and then she did the legwork. The first part of her job: writing up reports for her boss. But as time went on, she realized that the second part—getting in touch with project directors—wasn't getting done. Her boss stopped responding to her reports.

After analyzing the situation carefully, she discovered that instead of digesting the information and offering her opinion on the reports before she passed them on to her boss, she would give them to him with a note asking, "Which shall I get going on?" Her request required him to read through them and digest them himself, something he didn't have time for. She was avoiding the judgment part of the job because of its risks. Thus, in turn, her boss began to avoid her and her reports.*

> Quite honestly, people don't think about us as much as we think they do.

One way to seek truth in these situations is to conduct a self-evaluation (many tools are available) and then ask your senior pastor, director, or other colleague to take the same evaluation and answer the questions as if he or she were you. I've done this, and it was quite helpful. Even the feedback that was difficult to receive was helpful.

I also encourage you to counsel with a godly person as you go through this process so that he or she can help you to see those places in your life that are difficult to see. There are those of us who possess a natural tendency to be overresponsible and take ownership of others' issues, and then there are those of us who are underresponsible and blame others for our issues—neither of which is a good thing. Thus, the insights of another person are quite valuable to aid us in either accepting responsibility where we should or giving it to those to whom it belongs.

Now that we're in the electronic age, I've exchanged snail mail for e-mail, voice mail, and texting. It feeds the need in my soul to connect with others (although I could live a very useful life without a telephone). Yet I also enjoy pressing the "delete" key that allows me to easily eliminate junk mail, which makes me wonder, *Who empties the trash can in cyberspace?*

Fortunately, that's not my problem.

---

* Janice LaRouche and Regina Ryan, *Janice LaRouche's Strategies for Women* (New York: Avon, 1984), pp. 21, 22.

Dialogue Questions

1. What are some ways people form opinions about us? Which are legitimate? Which are not?

2. How much, and in what ways, are you influenced by what others think of you? Be honest.

3. If "being yourself" were to be liberating for you, how would you go about granting that same freedom to others?

4. Do you have a mentor with whom you can be totally yourself? Why or why not?

Chapter 10

Fingerprints of God

Lesson: God uses change to help us grow.

"Why don't *you* take my job?"
I met Kathy when she first began attending the Spencerville church. Out of that pastor–parishioner relationship we developed a strong friendship. When I left Spencerville to go to the General Conference, we became coworkers; she worked right down the hall from where I worked for the *Adventist Review*. She served as an editor in the Sabbath School/Personal Ministries Department.

We were sitting in her office one day in the winter of 2006 discussing her imminent move to Andrews University to complete her doctorate in religious education. We were brainstorming about who might be a good replacement for her. (Of course, a person doesn't usually get to choose his or her replacement, but it's always fun to speculate as to whom you'd like it to be.) In the course of our speculation session, she turned to me and asked, "Why don't *you* take my job?"

"What do you mean, *take your job?*" But the more she spoke about it, the more it seemed as though it might be a good fit. She asked if I would allow her to pass along my name to her directors. I told her I'd think about it.

Writing Is Life

I loved my job. Being an editor of the *Adventist Review* had been a dream come true for me. Someone once asked me, "You enjoy your work, don't you?" When I responded, "Yes," that person said, "I can tell. Your love of it comes through your writing."

There's something amazing about placing pen to paper (or fingers to computer keys) and mentally wrestling through the process of coming up with just the right word that will strike a chord in the hearts of its hearers. Some amused passersby laughed as they went by my office, watching me stare into space, trying to grab hold of a word as if it were coated with oil and slipping through my fingers. For some writers the process is merely endured as a means to get to the end: a finished product. However, I'm one of those glutton-for-punishment writers who enjoys the twists and the turns of the process, who crumples up the paper after a failed attempt at a thought, and still feels as if it were time well spent. I also loved the connection with the *Adventist Review* readers. To go to a local church and hear a church member say, "Oh, I read your writing. I especially enjoyed...," allowed me a chance to immediately connect and discuss topics related to us as Adventist Christians.

It isn't possible for me not to write. As one young writer explains it: "Some nights it seems that my heart doesn't pump blood through my veins, but words. They gather in my fingertips and pound on my hands until I let them fall out."[1] When I start my day with writing, the rest of my duties are done more efficiently. I'm more focused, and, quite honestly, I'm in a better mood. So it's best for those close to me if I allow the words to fall from my fingertips!

As I considered this move to the Sabbath School/Personal Ministries Department, it seemed as if God had some words for me. "Forget the former things; do not dwell on the past. See, I am doing a new thing! Now it springs up; do you not perceive it?" (Isa. 43:18, 19, NIV). I used to think of this solely as God encouraging the Israelites not to dwell on the sadness and oppression they were experiencing in exile and that He would deliver them. This perspective is correct, of course. But as I studied this verse more, I came to believe that God also used these words to encourage His people to move beyond even the former *good* things that He had done for them. It's as if He were saying, "My children, do not dwell on the former ways that I have delivered and guided you. Yes, remember them, but do not dwell on them. For today is a new day. I will lead you in a new way. If you continue to dwell on the past, you will miss My workings *now!* Do you understand what I am doing?"

Accepting this invitation to change jobs would allow me to broaden my skills as an editor. It would allow me to work with some of my best friends in the building. And it would allow me to continue to devote a portion of my time to writing.

The Etymology of Change

In the Chinese language, two words can be used to represent the term *crisis*: "danger" and "opportunity."[2] While this is true for the etymology of *crisis*, I think it's also true in the experience of change. Change can be difficult. And while change often means "danger" to a portion of our life experience, it can also bring priceless opportunities to our lives that we would never have dreamed of had we remained where we were: a new ministry opportunity, a new relationship, more leadership responsibilities, and so on.

It wasn't easy leaving a job I loved, people I cared for, and readers with whom I'd shared a part of my soul. I now understand that grief experts aren't making stuff up when they describe how people go through the various stages of grief when losing or leaving a job, similar to the death of a loved one or a divorce. Even though I chose to make my job change, it involved grieving. But I have come to believe that if we can go through life and adequately acknowledge our losses and do the hard work of grieving, it will bring healing, health, and wholeness to our lives.

> I learned that God is much bigger than I give Him credit for.

For one, I know many female pastors grieve because they have been denied an opportunity to exercise their pastoral calling, or they've had to leave a position because of unfairness or injustice. So how do we grieve "appropriately"? Well, I'm no expert on grief. However, besides experiencing my own grief as well as walking with many church members, family members, and friends through their grief journeys (I've conducted more funerals than any other church rite), I think I have a few things I can share:

First, I would encourage you to become familiar with the stages of grief, if you've not already done so: (1) shock and denial, (2) anger, (3) depression, (4) bargaining, (5) sadness, and (6) forgiveness. Even if you are familiar with them, review them. Elizabeth Kübler-Ross is the foremost expert on grief and has written some excellent books on the subject. Remember that grief is a process and the stages don't always come in linear fashion. Beyond a cognitive understanding of the subject, it's important to allow yourself to *experience* all the elements of grief. We're not always comfortable with anger, but it is an emotion present in the grief process that we must allow ourselves to experience. We must acknowledge it, deal with it, and then release it. Remember, too, that God can handle our anger. It's our indifference He doesn't like.

I remember leading a small group many years ago in which one of the members was a declared agnostic. We were talking about this subject of God being able to handle our anger, and he turned and said to me, "But if I were to express my anger at God, then I would have to *engage* Him." The thing is that God wants us to engage with Him. He wants us to come to Him with all of our emotions, including anger.

Second, I would encourage you to find a way to express your emotions. I've cried many tears over the death of my father as well as over the loss of dreams I've had in my life. There will come a time that the tears become less and the feelings associated with grief begin to diminish. And one day you'll realize that you're on the other side of the tunnel.

Third, I would encourage you to keep yourself physically healthy. We are wholistic beings, and our physical condition affects our emotional and spiritual condition, and vice versa. Eat well, rest, and seek stability and balance in this area of your life. It will be invaluable in your emotional and spiritual healing.

The Sameness of Change

I learned much through this process of change:

- I learned that God is patient; I am not.
- I learned that change can be an unwelcome houseguest upon its arrival but becomes a treasured family member the longer it remains.
- I learned that God is much bigger than I give Him credit for.
- I learned that God accomplishes His will in our lives through ways in which we never before dreamed.
- I learned that I am stronger than I thought, but I don't feel as strong as God thinks I am.
- I learned that a fulfilled life is more about what you bring to it than what it brings to you.
- I learned that truly all things work together for good to those who love God.

Not everyone in the workplace has the opportunity to be involved in the decision-making process to find his or her successor, although I think we'd be further ahead in the game if we utilized the predecessor's feedback. Whether we are the person leaving or the person arriving, we have much to learn in this process of change. But one thing is for sure: God is the God of yesterday, today, and forever (Heb. 13:8). You can trust Him with your past, your present, and your future. It's not that God will never change His ways of working in our lives. It's that His fingerprints will never change.

---

[1] Used with permission by Mary-Kate Spring Lee, Seasons Music, www.seasons music.com.

[2] Some people believe this to be untrue. However, a Chinese coworker of mine who speaks Mandarin Chinese confirmed it and says that it is true across the other Chinese dialects as well, regardless of pronunciation.

Dialogue Questions

1. List the jobs you've had over your lifetime. Which was your favorite? Why?

2. What motivates you to go to work each day: Getting a paycheck? Serving others? Doing your best? Being noticed? Is there one "right" answer?

3. When have you been given an opportunity to pursue a different vocation or increased responsibility? What did you leave behind? What challenges did you face?

4. How would a person know God is leading in a career choice? Or is that something God does for only pastors and teachers?

Chapter 11

Did He Say
What I Thought He Said?

Lesson: Anger is a God-given emotion.

If only he had said it once. But he said it twice—and even then he continued to elaborate.

Technology is great . . . when it works. During one of those why-can't-I-get-my-computer-to-run-faster-than-a-turtle days I called our tech department. As I stood next to my assistant's desk that afternoon working with her on a project, Gerald[1] showed up. I turned to look at him and exclaimed, "Wonderful! Thanks for coming so quickly."

He responded with a question: "You *do* know why your computer is running slow, don't you?" Before I responded, he answered his own question: "Because it's female."

I momentarily stood motionless, stunned. Did he just say what I thought he said? In a professional environment? I thought I'd give him a break since he was probably trying to be funny, so I turned to my assistant and said, laughing and shaking my head, "No, he didn't just say what I thought he said," and moved toward my office so we could check out my computer.

As I walked into my office, he continued: "No, I'm serious."

OK. This isn't funny anymore.

"Yeah, in my family my wife is the slow one," he said as he continued to elaborate.

Fortunately, he stopped the discussion about his wife. However, after taking a few minutes to look at my computer, he launched in again, speaking to me in a demeaning tone.

"Look at this! No wonder your computer is running slow." He pointed to an icon at the bottom of the screen. "You have more than 100 prompts that you've ignored. Why haven't you responded to these?"

I was no longer angry. I was livid.

"Gerald," I said to him in a slow, deliberate, controlled tone, "I would appreciate it very much if you would explain to me what I need to do so

that I can do it, instead of coming into my office and chastising me."
He told me what I needed to do and left. A fortunate decision for him.

Can a Christian Woman Be Angry?

Anger is taboo for many Christian women—*and* men, as a male friend
of mine reminded me as he read this chapter.

"Oh, we're not supposed to be angry. That's not a Christian thing to do."

"Why, I don't get angry. I just cry. That's OK."

"What? Get angry? Are you kidding? I'm stronger than that."

For many years I was one of those women who didn't get angry. I just
cried. That was much more of a society-approved response for a female.
However, even though most people would not have described me as an
angry woman, I held anger inside of me. Occasionally, if my husband said
something I didn't like, the anger surfaced. I didn't get angry by yelling
or screaming. I just looked at him with one of those "if looks could kill"
faces. He would say to me, "Sweetie, I don't like that look." I didn't do it
consciously. It just happened. Like those looks my dad gave me when I was
younger. No need to spank me. Just give me that look, and tears flowed
within seconds. Fortunately, in my 30s I realized that I needed to address
this stuffed anger, so I spent time working with a counselor in emotional
healing work.

I'm far from perfect, but I've learned much about anger—my own and
others. And I think the most important thing I've learned is that anger is
a God-given emotion; it's a signal that something going on is not right.
However, how it's handled determines its negative or positive potential.
Ephesians 4:26, 27 states it this way: "Go ahead and be angry. You do well
to be angry—but don't use your anger as fuel for revenge. And don't stay
angry. Don't go to bed angry. Don't give the Devil that kind of foothold in
your life" (Message).

In the book *Speaking the Truth in Love*, authors Ruth Koch and Kenneth
Haugk discuss anger in the context of assertiveness. I think that in order to
understand anger, it is helpful to define assertiveness.

As I said in chapter 5, assertive behavior is not aggressive behavior.
While aggressive behavior moves against others, and passive behavior
moves against self, *assertive behavior honors self while honoring others.*[2]
Thus, the question that arises for us in regard to assertiveness and anger
is "How can we express our anger while honoring ourselves and others,
without either denying the anger or being held captive by it? And in a way

that it will become a constructive force rather than a destructive force?"

Expressing and Receiving Anger

Here are a few guidelines that especially helped me over the years to express and receive anger in a healthy manner:

Own your anger

Owning one's anger means not wallowing in it. When a person can say "I feel angry" and identify the cause, it helps to dissipate it. Unconsciously, many people think that if they pretend that a problem doesn't exist, it will go away. Unfortunately, it doesn't work that way. The only thing that denial does is give more power to the problem.

When we "stuff" our anger, we risk its implosion. When it implodes, it can exhibit itself through such things as depression, addictions, feeling "stuck," or even physical ailments. We can also begin to misdirect our anger, taking it out on someone we love rather than dealing with the cause of the anger.

Use "I" messages

Boy, is this a tough one when you're in the thick of the battle! When you and your spouse are having an argument, it can be challenging to say, "Honey, I feel hurt when you tell me my dress makes me look like an elephant on steroids," when you really want to say, "Oh, yeah? Well, you don't exactly look like Tom Cruise yourself, buster!"

When Gerald came into my office that day, I think I came pretty close to using this principle: "I would appreciate it if you would explain to me what I need to do so I can do it, instead of coming into my office and chastising me." Because I really wanted to say, "You are such a jerk! Do you realize what a bad name you give men?" Besides not being very professional or loving, my saying that would have fed into the "aggressive woman" stereotype—you know, the description of a female canine animal.

Do not accept abuse

Anger is not a "bad" emotion; it is God-given feeling. Anger allows us to identify when someone is violating our boundaries—either physically or emotionally. Unfortunately, men and women who have been recipients of abuse don't always experience anger when they should. Or if they do, they minimize or deny the abuse.

Rose[3] was raised in an alcoholic home. However, she dreamed of going to college and working "for the church." She worked her way through college and eventually became a pastor. However, several years into her ministry she was experiencing difficulty with a few of her male colleagues. Nothing immoral or physically abusive took place. But when communication in these work relationships became strained, she sought to be intentional about addressing the problem—she went directly to the person, expressed her needs in an assertive manner, and used "I" messages. Nothing seemed to change. These colleagues either continued to ignore her, sabotage her work, shut her out of leadership "loops," yell at her, or put a "smoke screen" over her attempts to address the situation. Although she did everything in her power to heal the breach, she emerged from these relationships feeling responsible.

Rose made an appointment with a counselor and shared the details of these work relationships. She felt sadness about what had happened, questioning whether she could have done something more to make these relationships work. However, after hearing Rose tell her story, the counselor commented, "The thing I find amazing is that you are not angry with these people. You *should* be angry. How they treated you was wrong." While Rose wasn't blameless in these relationships, she came to realize that she had done all she could within these relationships and that their behavior toward her was actually abusive. Rose is learning to recognize these behavioral patterns. But she also continues to have others walk alongside her to help her see them more readily and more clearly.

Anger is taboo for many Christian women— *and* men.

Abuse is an important topic, and there is so much more that needs to be said, but it's outside the scope of this book. However, you should pay attention to your anger. Sometimes it has to do with something within our personality and character that we need to deal with. Other times it is a warning of the physical or emotional dangers of a situation. If you suspect you are in an abusive relationship, please seek out a trusted friend, pastor, or counselor with whom to talk.

Redemption

The bad news is that Gerald didn't express himself once but twice.

The good news is that twice was enough. A supervisor spoke with him about his unprofessional behavior. Fortunately, Gerald was open to change and began to act more professionally. I must admit that he became quite pleasant to deal with. He even stopped by my office occasionally to ask, "How can I be of help?" I hate to admit it, but my first (unspoken) response to his new question was *Did he say what I just thought he said?* He even asked this new question more than once.

I am no longer angry. I am grateful.

---

[1] Not his real name.

[2] R. Koch and K. Haugk, *Speaking the Truth in Love*, p. 23.

[3] Not her real name.

Dialogue Questions

1. List eight emotions (anger, happiness, frustration, etc.), then categorize them as *good* or *bad*. Which emotions, if any, are totally bad?

2. Repression is usually an unsatisfactory way to deal with negative emotions. What ways have you discovered to help you express your feelings in positive ways? Mention three.

3. Give some examples from your own life about the difference between being assertive and being aggressive. What is the border between one and the other?

4. Throughout history people have often turned their outrage or anger toward a cause that changed society. Think of at least five examples. What principles can we learn from them?

Chapter 12

Bold Words

Lesson: We have the power to change the world.

Did you ever imagine that God would use e-mail and Facebook to communicate with His people?

One day I received an e-mail from Fabi, a fellow minister, creative writer, and beautiful person whom I had the pleasure of working with for a time at the General Conference. She wrote:

"Bonita, I want to let you know that for the past few days I have been praying special, specific prayers for you. . . . Thank you for paving the way for other women and inspiring writers to break through barriers in our denomination. Thank you for all the risks you took and the tears you cried along the way. Thank you for working so hard, with so much integrity, grace, and passion in order to make the path smoother for women like me. Most of all, I have to thank you for your mentoring and your friendship. . . .

"So, Bonita, I encourage you, my sister. Please continue to make a solid difference wherever you are planted. Continue to allow God to blossom and stretch you. Continue to speak out boldly. Stand up for truth. . . .

"I can't wait to see what God is going to do with you next. Hold on, Bonita. . . . 'You ain't seen nothin' yet!' Your best days are still to come!

"I love you dearly. Fab."

Thank you, Fabi. I'm still trying to live up to your image of me.

She closed by referencing Deuteronomy 28:2: "You will experience all these blessings *if* you obey the Lord your God" (NLT).

Five days later another beautiful friend, Gemma, sent me a message through Facebook:

"Good morning, Bonita! I just prayed for you. Every day I pray for four FB friends whose pictures pop up to the left of my profile page, and I pray for them specifically. I prayed that God continues to give you wisdom and that He orders your steps—all the way—as you minister for Him. Thank you for standing for the truth. Have a wonderful week."

What a beautiful way to use Facebook to bless others!

God has used many godly people throughout my life to guide, encourage, *and* rebuke me. And I'm so grateful for their faithfulness and obedience to God and His messages to me through them.

"Bonita, *if* you remain faithful to Me and continue to walk obediently, you will continue to be a spiritual leader for My people. This isn't about you. You are dependent on *Me* for your spiritual strength."

"Bonita, trust Me. Work where you are planted, and allow Me to stretch and grow you. You may not always see it, but I am working in you and through you to make a difference in your life and in the lives of My people."

"Bonita, I've called you to stand up for truth. Not necessarily *your* truth, but *My* truth. Don't allow fear to keep you from the work to which I have called you. Don't let it keep you from speaking the bold words to which I have called you."

This may seem like a small order for *you*, but I know myself! I can be stubborn. I can be proud. I don't like controversy. (I've been told I'd make a great politician. I don't think it was a compliment.) But I also know that I don't have to accomplish the things God has called me to through my own power. It is *God's* power that will empower me to walk faithfully and obediently. It is *God's* power that will create in me the humility to stretch and grow. And it is *God's* power that will fill me with the courage to stand up for truth.

God wants to speak encouraging and bold words to you as well through these messages.

Walking Faithfully and Obediently

God calls you to walk faithfully and obediently. Jesus affirms in John 15:10 that it is through our obedience that we remain in the Father's love. Don't get this confused with salvation by works. Faith and trust precede obedience. If you remember in Exodus 20 when the commandments were given, the verse preceding the giving of them reads, "I am the Lord your God, who brought you out of the land of Egypt, out of the house of bondage" (Ex. 20:2, NKJV). The people weren't obeying in order to gain favor with God; they were obeying in response to God's favor and deliverance. Jesus didn't obey the Father in order to be called His Son. Jesus obeyed the Father because He was His Son. We don't obey to be accepted by the Father; we obey because we are accepted by the Father.

What is it that God is calling you to do? to be? We've come full circle from where we started in this book. Remember, this isn't about you. This isn't about what you are capable of as much as what God is capable of through you. It's scary to step out into unknown territory, but God has promised He will give us the strength to obey Him.

Blooming Where You Are Planted

God calls you to bloom where you are planted. Do you really trust that God is in control of your life? Do you trust that He will make all things work together for His good? Do you feel as though you're not making a difference in anyone's life? You're not the only one who feels this way. Often we have this idea that *if only* we were placed where we could do a "grand work" for God, then we'd be important to God and to others. However, often the "grand work" of God is to do the task at hand with integrity. And it is through this seemingly insignificant work that He will bring you through to the other side stronger than before.

Standing for Truth

God calls you to stand for truth. What is the truth for which you need to stand boldly? Of course, Jesus is the ultimate truth. And we all will be asked to take a bold stand in one way or another for Jesus and what He means to us. As pastors, we are called to speak God's Word truthfully. But there are other truths of His kingdom for which we must be bold and take a stand. Are you an accountant and need to stand up for truth in regard to financial matters in your organization? Are you a doctor and need to stand up against unethical practices that are threatening the lives of your patients? Are you a day-care provider and need to stand up for the child who's being abused? Remember, God is the God of justice, mercy, and compassion. And we are called to be His representatives.

Marching Orders

I believe that God also wants to speak encouraging and bold words to *us* through these messages.

Scripture tells us, "God created mankind in his own image, in the image of God he created them; male and female he created them" (Gen. 1:27, NIV). The image of God is not complete until male and female work together to more fully represent Him. *God's power working through us— men and women together—can change the world!* These are bold words of truth that we must stand up for as a church.

We can change the world! Satan knows this. Satan knows that if men and women work together faithfully and obediently, valuing the other without undermining or blaming each other, allowing themselves to be stretched and grown, and courageously speaking the truth of God's kingdom through our words and actions, God's power will become even more evident in a world that so desperately needs a vision of something more than what it is.

But it won't happen by merely wishing it into existence. Men and women must humble themselves and open themselves up to learning from each other. These new relationships will require humility, acceptance, and a willingness to speak truth lovingly and faithfully. We must form partnerships to transmit knowledge, wisdom, and support relevant to work, career, or even Christian experience. Within church and corporate worlds, these mentoring-type relationships take place effortlessly between young male protégés and older, more experienced men. But generally, for women, they rarely take place; this requires more intentionality, starting now.

I am encouraged by the male leadership of the North American Division who are stepping up to the plate and boldly speaking out for women in ministry. I especially applaud my brothers in Christ for their willingness to take this risk to stand up for justice, to faithfully speak bold words of truth, and to encourage and partner with women in ministry to fulfill their God-given calling.

> God's power working through us—men and women together—can change the world!

This partnership makes the devil tremble! My hope is that our church will use this time to come together for dialogue and mutual respect.

Who could have imagined that God would use e-mail and Facebook to communicate a message to His people? Can you imagine God using men and women partnering together to communicate a message to His people and to the world?

For me, the fulfillment of that vision is worth living in a man's world.

Dialogue Questions

1. What methods—either new or old-fashioned—do you use to encourage others? Why those?

2. God uses a variety of people to help, encourage, and affirm us. Whom did God use this week to speak encouragement or affirmation to you? What was His message to you?

3. What bold words has God spoken to you lately? How have you acted on them?

4. How can we live these principles more faithfully? What would your workplace, church, and world look like if men and women faithfully partnered to accomplish the work at hand?

Appendix

Ordination Is Not the Issue:
Reflections of a Female Pastor

Bonita Joyner Shields

First published in *Adventist Today,* Winter 2009
I sat staring at my computer screen, stunned. After a few moments my disbelief morphed into tears. It probably wasn't the first time a seminary student sat crying at her computer over a homework assignment! Regardless, it may have been a first with the source of such an emotional response having come from reading the works of an early church father.

The term *early church fathers* refers to the early and influential theologians and writers in the Christian church, particularly those of the first five centuries of Christian history. Some of the most recognizable names include Ignatius, Polycarp, Origen, John Chrysostom, and Augustine. But Tertullian was the one who tore at my soul.

My encounter with this man who lived in a totally different time and place, many centuries ago, brought me face to face with the here-and-now and revealed to me a somber truth: our church's resistance to female spiritual leadership and its refusal to ordain women into pastoral ministry are merely symptoms of a deeper issue. Until we address this deeper issue, I believe ordination is a moot point.

Something to Cry About
The writings of these early church theologians are typically placed in three categories: Ante-Nicene Fathers, Nicene Fathers, and Post-Nicene Fathers.[1] Tertullian, an Ante-Nicene Father, considered the founder of Italian Christianity, wrote in the second and third centuries. Tertullian, who so eloquently expounded theological doctrines about the Resurrection, the nature of Christ, and the Trinity, had this to say to a female audience:

"And do you not know that you are (each) an Eve? The sentence of God on this sex of yours lives in this age: the guilt must of necessity live too. *You* are the devil's gateway: *you* are the unsealed of that (forbidden) tree: *you* are the first deserter of the divine law: *you* are she who persuaded him whom the devil was not valiant enough to attack. *You* destroyed so easily God's image, man. On account of *your* desert—that is, death—even the Son of God had to die. And do you think about adorning yourself over and above your tunics of skins?"[2]

Tertullian wasn't alone in his views. Augustine, a Latin theologian and bishop of Hippo, believed that males represent the mind, while females represent the concupiscent (sexual) nature.[3] Aphrahat, a Christian Assyrian author of the fourth century—and possibly influenced by Tertullian—wrote that "from the beginning it was through woman that the adversary had access unto men . . . for she is the weapon of Satan. . . . For because of her the curse of the Law was established."[4] John Chrysostom, a late-fourth-century theologian, commented on the text in Matthew 19 (stating that it is good not to marry) with these words:

"What else is woman but a foe to friendship, an unescapable punishment, a necessary evil, a natural temptation, a desirable calamity, a domestic danger. . . Therefore if it be a sin to divorce her when she ought to be kept, it is indeed a necessary torture; for either we commit adultery by divorcing her, or we must endure daily strife."[5]

Basil of Caesarea, also a fourth-century theologian, spoke about a husband's treatment of his wife: "However hard, however fierce a husband may be, the wife ought to bear with him. . . . He strikes you, but he is your husband. . . . He is brutal and cross, but he is henceforth one of your members, and the most precious of all."[6]

These views were not confined to the early church. In the fifteenth century Heinrich Kraemer and Jacob Sprenger wrote a training manual for neophyte inquisitors in their pursuit of squelching witchcraft. Under the section titled "Why Superstition Is Chiefly Found in Females," they offered numerous reasons for this belief. One reason was that females are more carnal than males—especially since "there was a defect in the formation of the first woman, since she was formed from a bent rib." Another reason is that "females are intellectually like children." Still another reason cited was that "when a woman thinks alone, she thinks evil." Thus, the writers came to the following conclusion: "All witchcraft comes from carnal lust, which is in females insatiable."[7]

These views, and many like them, form the history of the Christian church. And while today I doubt many people would overtly express these views, do we think that these views made no impression on their readers—especially since such influential theologians espoused them? Do we think that these views have not been transmitted through the "spiritual DNA" of the Christian church? Do we think that by merely granting a credential of ordination to women that we will supplant these deeply entrenched, albeit often unconscious, beliefs that women are (spiritually) inferior to men? that women bear the entire responsibility of sin for the human race? that men are symbols of intelligence while women are, well, *sex symbols*?

Tertullian and the other early church theologians demonstrate that the issues regarding women in ministry in our church go much deeper than ordination. The deeper issue is the devaluation of the female image of God.

It Didn't Start With Tertullian

The belief systems of these theologians were not formed in a vacuum. This devaluation of girls and women is seen throughout secular history— especially in the form of female infanticide. Archaeological studies of infant remains conducted in ancient Rome revealed that "most infants died around birth. This along with the fact that these individuals were disposed of in the sewer rather than given regular burial was interpreted as evidence for infanticide. . . . When such societies practice infanticide, more girls than boys are likely to be victims."[8] This practice continues in various countries even today.

The point of all of these illustrations is not to prove that all males are bad and all females are victims. Their purpose is to reveal how far humanity has gone in trampling the feminine image of God underfoot.

The first chapter of Scripture states, "Let *us* make mankind [Heb. *adam*, man, mankind] in our image, in our likeness, so that *they* may rule over the fish of the sea. . . . So God created mankind in his own image, in the image of God he created them; male and female he created them" (Gen. 1:26, 27, NIV).

It takes both male and female to most accurately reflect the image of God. Unfortunately, God's people haven't always embraced and valued this image. What more somber, painful image do we need of God's people devaluing females than to picture the concubine of Judges 19 *willingly* being offered up by her husband to be sexually violated and fatally abused by a mob of perverted males? Or the early church theologians who continue to blame the first woman for their sins? Or the Adventist man today who finds no discrepancy between loving his wife as Christ loves the church and beating her?

God's people need to create a community that will cease to condone the oppression and abuse of women—physically, emotionally, and spiritually—by its writings, attitudes, and silence. God's people need to create a renewed vision of men and women working together and building each other up, representing more fully the image of God. God's people need to create a partnership between men and women to spread the gospel—without worrying about who's to blame for this mess we're in!

Men and Women in Partnership

How do we go about creating a renewed vision of male–female relationships in the church? There are no easy answers, but I would like to offer a few reflections on how I see us taking steps in that direction.

Accept responsibility for our own actions.

The writings of Tertullian and other early theologians reveal that they viewed women as mentally and spiritually inferior, thus continuing to blame women for bringing sin into the world and for any temptations men experienced in their relationships with women. But this is what the tempter wants. He wants to divert our attention away from the true source of blame. A common phrase in our society is "The devil made me do it." Well, at least we're going in the right direction with the blame! Ultimately, however, it stops with us.

Many reasons exist for why blame and oppression take place in our world—and in our church. One of those reasons is fear. And I believe that this fear is the underlying motivation behind the words of many of these early church theologians. We often ridicule, belittle, or seek to avoid those people or things we fear the most. One man shared his fear regarding the dynamics of working with women: "I don't think you understand the pull that men feel in relation to women. When I feel that pull, I just have to run because I'm not sure what would happen if I didn't. And isn't that what the Bible says—to flee temptation? I don't know what else to do with everything that I feel."[9]

This pull, this attraction, is real and often difficult for both men and women. But I believe if we can create safe places in the body of Christ where we can openly discuss these struggles together, we can thereby remove the power of the "secret." By doing so, we could then accept our humanness, help each other with these struggles, and in the power of *agape* love, men can partner with women in ministry. "For God has not given us a spirit of fear, but of power and of love and of a sound mind" (2 Tim. 1:7, NKJV).[10]

Women are by no means responsible for these struggles that men experience. But we must also accept responsibility for our actions. As sisters in Christ we can make choices that do not add to men's struggles in their relationships with us; for example, we can dress modestly rather than immodestly, be authentic rather than manipulate through the power of our gender, and view men as partners and brothers in Christ rather than "us against them."[11]

Confront the stereotypes and prejudices about women

I once shared a book about ministering in the local church with a female colleague. After reading it, she offered up an honest and insightful commentary. She said, "Bonita, as I was reading the book, I thought to myself, *This is excellent!*" After she had gotten about three quarters through the book, however, she read the back of the book to discover that the author was a woman. She continued, "I'm embarrassed to say that when I discovered the gender of the author, even as a woman I began to discount her words." The view of women as being mentally and spiritually inferior is not confined to the male gender. Unfortunately, women have also embraced this heresy. Could it be that in addition to the prejudices and fears that men bring to the table women bring their own set of prejudices and fears?

"There is no longer Jew or Greek, there is no longer slave or free, there is no longer male and female; for all of you are one in Christ Jesus" (Gal. 3:28, NRSV). Paul undoubtedly makes this threefold affirmation in response to the threefold distinction male Jews would utter in the morning prayers at the time: "I thank God that I am not a Gentle, a slave, or a woman."[12]

This text hits at the heart of ethnic, socioeconomic, and gender societal prejudices. The Adventist view relegates this text to merely the equality of salvation for these groups of people.[13] But I believe it goes deeper than that. If God calls us to manifest this new paradigm in church fellowship, does it not seem logical that it would also manifest itself in church politics? If we are to truly live out this principle in the body of Christ, we need to choose spiritual leadership based on spiritual qualifications rather than societal status. For example, the local professional (i.e., doctor, lawyer) would not be chosen as head elder merely because of his social standing in society. The local janitor of that medical office or law firm may be gifted with spiritual leadership. If they belong to the same church, the professional would then be submitting to the spiritual leadership of someone "below" them socially. *That's* the radical nature of the gospel![14]

However, in our current paradigm of church politics, besides seeing the opposite of the above scenario taking place often, we exclude women because we confuse male headship in marriage—as God has called us to—with male headship of the church. *Christ* is the head of the church! Female spiritual leadership in the body of Christ does not negate the male headship of the marriage.

Interpret Scripture through the lens of the gospel and responsible hermeneutics

I listened to an Adventist evangelist share his views on women in ministry. He strung together texts in Scripture that on the surface appear to exclude women from certain roles. The pastor then said, "These aren't *my* words; I'm just telling you what's in Scripture." I find that to be an irresponsible use of God's Word.

Scripture is not a book from which to pull proof texts in order to prove our theological position. These were living documents given to living persons to reconcile them into a living relationship with a living God. As such, they must be understood within the *context* of that relationship in order to know how they are to apply to our lives today. Scripture has been (mis)used to "prove" some heinous things in human history. A little more than 150 years ago Christians were quoting Scripture to support slavery as God's plan for society.

It's not in the scope of this work to discuss the theological arguments against women in ministry. However, one example of our not viewing Scripture through Christological eyes is the argument of rejecting women in ministry because the Old Testament priests were men. However, these priests were types of Christ, the ultimate high priest as revealed in the book of Hebrews, and thus they needed to be male. Yet if we were to take that argument to its logical and consistent conclusion, all male pastors today would be required to submit to a physical examination prior to ordination, as did the Old Testament priests (see Lev. 21). This means that no man could be a pastor if he were bald, had unkempt hair, was a dwarf, performed funerals (because dead people are there), etc.—the list gets *worse!*

If we are to interpret what God's Word means for us today, we must confront our prejudices and biases, we must seek to discover what God's Word meant to the original audience, and we must seek to read it through Christological eyes.

A New Paradigm

Ellen White comments on Galatians 3:28 as follows: "It was not the apostle's work to overturn arbitrarily or suddenly the established order of society. To attempt this would be to prevent the success of the gospel. But he taught principles which struck at the very foundation of slavery and which, if carried into effect, would surely undermine the whole system."[15]

Within the context of Galatians 3:28, I believe these words can also be applied to race, class, or gender. Jesus had women within His inner circle of followers. Paul labored side by side with women in spreading the gospel.[16] They lived and taught the gospel principles that strike at the very foundation of the devaluation of women and that, *if carried into effect,* could surely undermine the whole belief system.

Can you imagine a community of faith in which we empowered men and women by our writings, attitudes, and voices? in which men and women strengthened each other for the work of the gospel? in which men and women partnered in ministry to give the world a more complete picture of God? in which everyone in the priesthood of all believers is ordained for ministry? in which Tertullian will no longer have the power to bring us to tears?

I want to be part of that community.

---

[1] "Nicene" is the adjective that describes the ecumenical church council held in Nicaea in Bithynia (part of present-day Iznik in Turkey) in A.D. 325. This council was convened by Constantine and included 318 bishops—one sixth of all the bishops of the empire. Next to the Apostolic Council at Jerusalem, it has been called the most important and illuminative of all the councils of Christendom.

[2] Augustine, *The Nicene and Post-Nicene Fathers,* Vol. III, p. 523.

[3] *Ibid.*

[4] Aphrahat, *Nicene and Post-Nicene Fathers of the Christian Church,* Vol. XIII, Part II, p. 367.

[5] Denis R. Janz, ed., *A Reformation Reader* (Minneapolis: Fortress Press, 1999).

[6] Basil of Caesarea, *The Hexaemeron,* Homilies 1 and 7, p. 93.

[7] *Ibid.*

[8] Simon Mays and Marina Faerman, "Sex Identification in Some Putative Infanticide Victims From Roman Britain Using Ancient DNA," *Journal of Archaeological Science* 28 (2001): 555–559, doi:10.1006/jasc.2001.0616.

[9] R. H. Barton, *Equal to the Task,* p. 51.

[10] For an excellent treatment of the topic of men and women partnering in the power of love rather than fearing our sexuality, see Barton's *Equal to the Task.*

[11] For a fuller treatment of this aspect of men and women partnering as brothers and sisters in Christ, see Sarah Sumner's *Men and Women in the Church* (Downers Grove, Ill.: InterVarsity Press, 2003).

[12] F. F. Bruce, *The Epistle to the Galatians, New International Greek Testament*

Commentary (Grand Rapids: Eerdmans, 1982), p. 187.

[13] *The Seventh-day Adventist Bible Commentary* (Washington, D.C.: Review and Herald Pub. Assn., 1953-1957), vol. 6, p. 962.

[14] For a discussion on what it would look like for Jews and Gentiles to be "one in Christ," see the commentary on Galatians 3:28 in Bruce.

[15] Ellen G. White, *The Acts of the Apostles* (Mountain View, Calif.: Pacific Press Pub. Assn., 1911), p. 459.

[16] See Mark 15:40, 41; Luke 24:22; 1 Corinthians 16; and 3 John as a few examples.